17 HABITS TO HELP HIGH ACHIEVERS
SURVIVE & THRIVE IN LEADERSHIP & LIFE

YOUR
OXYGEN MASK
FIRST

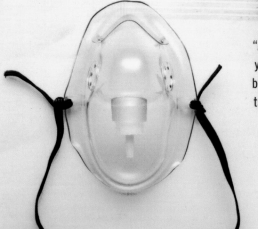

"A stark reminder that
you can't take care of
business until you first
take care of yourself."
—**LIZ WISEMAN,**
bestselling author
of *Multipliers* and
Rookie Smarts

KEVIN N. LAWRENCE

PRAISE

"*Your Oxygen Mask First* is a stark reminder that you can't take care of business until you first take care of yourself. Lawrence's playbook offers a rich set of practices to help you achieve success with no regrets."

—LIZ WISEMAN, bestselling author of *Multipliers* and *Rookie Smarts*

"Kevin has locked arms with my growth firm, Medix, for more than seven years and has consistently challenged our personal and professional leadership limits! His actionable tools turned out to be truly invaluable resources to our organization and helped allow us to scale as leaders. I encourage you to read and use this book as a resource for your professional and personal growth!"

—ANDREW LIMOURIS, President and CEO, Medix

"If you're looking for practical wisdom from a battle-tested field general of business coaching—look no further. This step-by-step guide enables CEOs to tap into their hidden wells of greatness—redefining success as much more than a healthy balance sheet."

—VERNE HARNISH, Founder of Entrepreneurs' Organization (EO) and author of *Scaling Up* (Rockefeller Habits 2.0)

"This isn't the normal business blather. If you are serious about growing yourself as well as growing your business, Kevin's book is invaluable. These tools are the best collection I've seen. They are practical and exceptionally helpful for any high achiever looking to grow and improve. If you just take one of these tools and practice it regularly, I have no doubt you'll improve your life and your business."

—BEN GODSEY, President and CEO, ProService Hawaii

"*Your Oxygen Mask First* flies in the face of what we've been taught about achieving success. Kevin shines light on the fallacy that being successful at work is the be-all and end-all, while giving his readers the strength, clarity, and confidence to make rapid and insightful changes."

—ANKUR GUPTA, Joint Managing Director, Ashiana Housing Ltd.

"If you're looking for practical wisdom on how the middle path between the selfless leader and the genius iconoclast can lead to greatness, pick up this book."

—KAIHAN KRIPPENDORFF, author of *Outthink the Competition*

"One of the biggest challenges for a highly successful leader in a growth company is motivating yourself on a regular basis. Kevin hit it out of the park with ideas and tools to help motivate me for a lifetime!"

—BRENT PARENT, CEO, Material Handling Services

"Kevin has been coaching CEOs and their teams for close to 20 years— he's one of the best in the biz—and his content in *Your Oxygen Mask First* is a must-read for any leader today."

—CAMERON HEROLD, Founder of COO Alliance and author of *Double Double, Meetings Suck* and *The Miracle Morning for Entrepreneurs*

"I have been working with Kevin since 2003. Kevin has helped me move through the asteroid belt of my life. He stopped me from selling my company for $1.00 to go to sell T-shirts on the beach and encouraged me to keep my business, setting it up the way I wanted, allowing me to grow it and leverage it to do good in the world. I now have the freedom that all entrepreneurs dream of, and I am able to spend quality time with my family and work only on things I enjoy and that bring great meaning to my life. I owe everything to Kevin."

—NIGEL BENNETT, Founder of Aqua-Guard and author of *Take that Leap – An Entrepreneur's Ride Through the Universe*

"Having known, observed and worked with Kevin for over a decade, he has masterfully developed 17 habits for successful leaders to find their 5th gear of performance, satisfaction and impact...practical principles and tools to grow in areas often unaddressed, even by the most effective leaders."

—KEITH CUPP, CEO Gazelles International Coaching Association

"There are books that are a philosophy and then books that are a roadmap. This is a book that combines the two and gives CEOs a practical step-by-step action plan to being world class performers."

—PETER BOOLKAH, The Transition Guy

"I have fun (not all of the time) working with Kevin Lawrence to achieve outrageous success, that being defined differently for everyone. If it were not for this straightforward, direct, driven and passionate guy pushing and prodding and cutting through the B.S., my Partners and I would not be where we are today. Not perfect, but 90% of where we want to be. I am not surprised at the title or content of Kevin's book...it cuts through the crap of daily business decisions and offers no-nonsense, direct advice. Oxygen is what you need in business, so you'd better be prepared to don the oxygen mask periodically to achieve outrageous success (and to get you through Kevin's direct and boisterous book)."

—CASEY LANGBROEK, Partner, Langbroek, Louwerse & Thiessen

"*Your Oxygen Mask First* challenged me to look in the mirror and consider what it takes to be authentically successful. It provided not only a clear *why*, but also the *how* in highly practical steps. The seventeen habits provide a life-changing framework that has ever-increasing circles of influence as they are implemented."

—HAZEL JACKSON, CEO, Biz Group

"*Your Oxygen Mask First* completely crushes core beliefs about success. Through his compelling and provoking approach, Kevin Lawrence proves that you can have astounding success in all areas of your life—but first you have to do the unthinkable. As a leader, you have to put yourself first—a revolutionary concept that confronts beliefs, experiences, and often egos! But it's a concept that powerfully changes lives. Kevin not only shows how to master this approach in easy, practical steps, but he also provides the confidence to make immediate changes to turbo-boost your life. It's a must-read for anyone wanting to bring their head and heart together and to truly have it all."

—SUE HOLLIS, Co-founder The TravelEdge Group Australia

"A refreshingly authentic and practical tool kit, *Your Oxygen Mask First* is a must-read for all leaders. There is a way to triumph—to be successful at work—without delaying your life!"

—MICHELLE LAVALLEE, Certified Topgrading® Coach

"This book is different: no fluff, but instead practical advice and provocative questions from a seasoned pro. Every chapter delivers insights that help me to reflect on what's important in my life—and then to focus directly on the goals to get me there. This is a great book!"

—DAVE MINHAS, Managing Partner, Pivotal LLP

"This book is a must-read for each and every person committed to leading, living, and working an exceptional life. I highly recommend reading this book, but more importantly, following Kevin's process to create, and sustain, success beyond business itself."

—DAVE BANEY, Author of *The 3x5 Coach*

"Coach Kevin regularly works with the CEOs and senior leaders of some of the fastest-growing midmarket companies in the world. In this book, he shares insights on how he has helped high-growth leaders who confront and overcome many of the personal and professional challenges of real-world leadership. His exercises are simple, powerful, and impactful. Read this book, and you will learn better ways to lead, and better ways to live life."

—DOUG DIAMOND, Business Improvement LLC

"This is probably the most honest and practical business book that I've read! Lawrence unashamedly confronts the brutal facts surrounding the real-life "success trap" many entrepreneurs find themselves in. This book contains no BS and is packed with simple explanations and actionable tools to enable you to live your life fully while running your company successfully."

—HAYLEY ERNER, Advisor and Confidant to CEOs

"This is the best book I have read for entrepreneurial CEOs. And it's one they will actually read: short and to the point. Lawrence clearly knows the traps of owning a business and how to get out of them. This is a must-read for anyone with a growing business."

—NAN O'CONNOR, Master Certified Coach

"I was fortunate that my path crossed with Coach Kevin's more than thirteen years ago. I was in a dark place in my life despite the fact that everything appeared to be all right on the surface. My business was doing very well, but my success was not bringing me as much joy and satisfaction, if any, as I thought it would. Kevin helped me discover that I needed to take care of myself first, follow my passions, and get rid of my demons by facing them head on. It hasn't happened overnight, and it is an ongoing process, but it's one that I embrace.

I am able to use Kevin's feedback, tools, and techniques as a compass to make the best possible decisions to stay on course in my business and in my life. I approach this journey with gratitude, excitement, passion, and a hunger for what's to come. I no longer measure my wealth in dollars and cents. Instead, I now measure it by the amount of precious time I am able to spend with my loved ones, making memories that are absolutely priceless!"

—VINCE D'AGOSTINO, President, Mayfield Financial Services

"I have been fortunate enough to become one of those loved ones that Vince mentioned in the previous blurb. It has been an amazing experience to watch Vince on his journey to become the best person that he can be. Our relationship would not be what it is today had he not started on this journey thirteen years ago. Thank you, Kevin, for being such an inspiring and guiding force in our lives. I know this book will be a huge success because I see what your processes and techniques have done for us. It made not only Vince strive to be a better person, but also everyone around him!"

—DIANA NADINIC

"We have been working directly with Kevin for almost four years with amazing results. Kevin's business insights, experience, and disciplined approach have had a major impact on the performance of our company. Not only have we seen an increase in business results, but with his guidance we are continuously improving our systems and practices for long-term stability and growth."

—DAVE KEARNS, General Manager & Paul Kearns President,
Fossil Project Services Ltd.

"When I began the adventures of business, I didn't realize it would consume as much of me as I allowed. Thankfully I read *My Oxygen Mask First*, which has helped me to be more happy, more healthy, and a better husband and father. The amazing thing is that this discipline also makes me a more effective leader in my businesses."

—DANNY CHASE, President, Chase Office Interiors

YOUR OXYGEN MASK FIRST

17 Habits to Help High Achievers Survive
& Thrive in Leadership & Life

ISBN   978-1-61961-783-4   Paperback

        978-1-61961-784-1   Ebook

LIONCREST
PUBLISHING

17 HABITS TO HELP HIGH ACHIEVERS
SURVIVE & THRIVE IN LEADERSHIP & LIFE

YOUR
OXYGEN MASK
FIRST

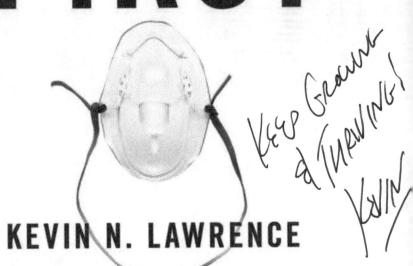

KEVIN N. LAWRENCE

KEEP GROWING & THRIVING!
Kevin

CONTENTS

For my family who always supports my crazy ventures,
and for my clients who always challenge me to learn.

— ACKNOWLEDGEMENTS —

Mentors & Teachers

I extend my gratitude and respect to the remarkable people who have guided me along my own leadership journey. I consider myself lucky to know you. It all started with Norm and Lois Lawrence (also called Dad and Mom) and Betty Howatt (my Grandma), and then continued on with Matt Jamieson, Joff Grohne, Warren Morgan, Teresia LaRocque, Thomas Leonard, Greg Clowminzer, Nan O'Connor, Verne Harnish, Ron Huntington, Jim Collins and Obaid Al Tayer.

Book Contributors & Supporters

People talk about how it takes a village to raise a child. I discovered the same to be true for writing a book. Thank you to all of these helpful people, in alphabetical order.

Carolynn Arthur, Andrew Barber Starkey, Karen Beattie, Nigel Bennett, Peter Boolkah, Ed Capaldi, Danny Chase, Keith Cupp, Hazel Jackson, Steve Dale-Johnson, Nicole Davis, Doug Diamond, Hayley Erner, Jay Evans, David Greer, Ian Hills, Sue Hollis, Casey Langbroek, Michelle LaVallee, Norm and Lois Lawrence, Andrew Limouris, Julie Prescott, Mary Rezek, Dean Ritchey, Angela Santiago, Mark Smiciklas, Richard Vann.

A very special thanks to Jacqueline Voci who has been my writing partner and editor on this book – I could not have done it without your insights and determination.

And, last but certainly not least, Janice Watkins, who works tirelessly to help me do great work for our clients. Her unwavering support helps me be the best I can.

Family

Enough cannot be said about the amazing people I call family. The wild and adventurous life I live is made rich by my travelling companions. Thank you to my wife Angela, son Brayden, and daughter Ashley.

———— PREMISE ————

"Life should not be a journey to the grave with the intention of arriving safely in a pretty and well preserved body, but rather to skid in broadside in a cloud of smoke, thoroughly used up, totally worn out, and loudly proclaiming, "Wow! What a Ride!"

HUNTER S. THOMPSON, Journalist & Author

Most Advice is Nonsense

There are a billion leadership books on the market, so you might be wondering: why bother with this one? I wrote this book because the exasperating truth is that most advice offered to business leaders is complete nonsense.

Too many well-meaning authors regurgitate ideas that, in my experience, just don't match the practical circumstances of leaders.

It's not that these writers are entirely wrong—their advice might work well for normal, everyday people. But high-achievers have unique needs that require a distinct way of thinking.

For the past twenty years I've specialized in helping CEOs, executives and other high-achievers survive success so they can take on bigger and bigger challenges. I've helped them thrive, not just professionally but personally. Along the way I've studied and tested most every leadership theory known to humankind.

This book is a concise but far-reaching summary of the best information and tools I've discovered in two decades of coaching and advising. I set out to deliver it to you with no holds barred.

It's my nature to tell it like it is. I don't mince words. I don't break news gently. I say what needs to be said, even when the truth is uncomfortable. Consider this a disclaimer.

The Upside of the Dichotomy

In case you haven't already noticed, leadership is a completely crazy way to spend your life. But it's also ridiculously amazing, and that's the dichotomy.

The upside of leadership is that your life is exhilarating and rewarding beyond belief. You build the magical things you dream up in your mind.

You test your personal limits, and experience huge, unimaginable wins that make you feel like you're standing on the peak of Everest.

You meet fascinating people and build lifelong relationships that inform how you see the world.

Whether it's a start-up in your garage, a division of a multinational, a family business you've inherited—or any other situation—leadership is all consuming, and changes you forever.

In the end, if you've done it right, you'll leave this world a little or a lot better than you found it.

That's what I call a life worth living.

The Dark Side of the Dichotomy

People rarely talk about the dark side of leadership.

The harsh truth is, leadership can crush people made of steel.

You experience moments so intense you seriously wonder if you will make it out alive—much less with your business intact.

The pressure can seem so unbearable you question why you chose this life in the first place. At times, the weight of your company feels like it's bearing down on you. You need to make gut-wrenching decisions that affect people's lives and careers.

In these moments you wonder if you have the stomach for it all. You question your intelligence, your capacity—and, in the very darkest hours– even your sanity.

Elvis

My fascination with the dichotomy of leadership began on a summer day in 1977 when the music icon of a generation, Elvis Presley, died at the early age of 42. I was a kid at the time, but hearing that news hit me hard.

I couldn't understand how someone with everything to live for could self-destruct with so much life left to live. It made no sense.

As I grew up, I often reflected on amazing people who were crushed by success and wondered what the heck went wrong. People like Marilyn Monroe, Janis Joplin, Jimmy Hendrix and Kurt Cobain puzzled and fascinated me.

I always felt there had to be an explanation, an avoidable cause. I wanted to know the secret to achieving huge success, without being clobbered by it.

Eventually I made it my mission, and my career, to make sense of the leadership dichotomy. I committed myself to understanding why some people triumph while others get trampled.

After two decades of research and observation I can tell

you the difference has almost nothing to do with talent, drive or perseverance.

It all comes down to this: *If you buy into the myth of martyrdom, you will be pummelled by your own success.*

The Myth of Martyrdom

You probably believe there is literally *no* time in your life to take proper care of yourself, to indulge in activities that are just for you, and you alone.

You believe as a leader, a spouse, a parent, a community organizer —whatever combination of roles you play—that these roles far outweigh your own personal needs.

You are conditioned to believe this is what adulthood looks like, what leadership looks like.

This is the myth of martyrdom; the dark lie that makes leaders feel guilty for having human needs.

But it is *impossible* to steer a company to its greatest potential if you aren't in your strongest state as an individual.

So if you ever feel profoundly depleted or distressed by your business, it's not a sign to slow down or walk away. It's a sign that you're suffocating and need a new approach to survive success.

There is no in-between with leadership. It either it slowly destroys your life or it forces you to get stronger.

You Need Oxygen

The solution is simple: you need oxygen. And lots of it. All the time.

In a plane crisis, you must don your own mask first so you have the oxygen to survive and help others. Your first instinct might be to leap into rescue mode, but you're of no use to anyone if you can't breathe.

Leadership is no different. You need to put yourself first. You need to be selfish.

Now, you need to know I don't define selfishness as manipulating every situation to your own benefit.

This is about giving yourself permission to put yourself first. It's about making your needs an unwavering priority, so you are strong and resilient enough to be of service to others.

It may seem like you can expend every ounce of your energy on your business and the people you care about, but this short-sighted view is the exact reason so many leaders crash and burn.

You're Getting Squeezed Out

Most leaders see the world in two categories of 'work' and 'life', with 'life' being a catch-all for everything that isn't business. 'Life' usually represents all of the people and causes outside of work that matter to you.

But hang on. Something crucial is totally getting squeezed out...what is it? Ah yes, *you*. *You're* getting squeezed out.

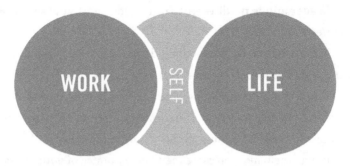

Remember when you were in your teens and early 20s? You probably had a ton of time and energy to spend on things that mattered just to you and you alone. To explore your fascinations. To do the things you love.

Then adulthood happened. Leadership happened. Family happened. And 'self' started to feel like a dirty word because of those other priorities. So it got relegated to the background. You were conditioned to believe that's what mature, responsible people do.

The reality is, you can only shut out your 'self' for so long until the self-neglect suffocates you. It affects your business performance, your family life...everything.

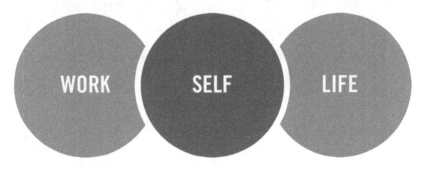

The only solution is to add that extremely crucial 'self' category back into your reality.

If you ignore your own well-being, the smartest business strategy on the planet can't save you.

But if you learn the proper tools for coping with the massive life you've chosen, your potential is unending.

How to Use This Book

This book can be used in different ways, depending on your personality. You might choose to read it all the way through, and then go back to work through the habits and exercises, chapter by chapter, or in order of personal priority.

You may prefer to take each chapter as it comes, reading it, absorbing it, doing the exercises, taking the time to incorporate the habit into your life.

There is no right or wrong.

One thing is universal: mastering the habits in this book is a lifelong journey. You can perpetually take each one deeper and deeper.

I encourage you to use this book as an ongoing resource for your evolution as a leader. Revisit the chapters as new challenges arise in your life.

Here are five things to know:

1. Don't be overwhelmed. This is a concise book but it packs a punch and covers a lot of territory. You're not meant to absorb and understand everything in one reading.

2. Each chapter presents one habit and offers a set of steps to help you understand and adopt the habit. You must actually _do_ these steps to get any results. They aren't just ideas to contemplate.

3. Pay close attention to the 'Gut Check' section at the end of each chapter where you rate your abilities. Even if you give yourself a '10', do the steps in the chapter anyway. You can only get stronger.

4. You can access a free _Your Oxygen Mask First_ toolkit at: _lawrenceandco.com/books_

5. Stay tuned for a list of resources and my top book recommendations at the end of the book.

There's More Where This Came From: Sign Up

If this book speaks to you, you can receive succinct, hard-hitting insights on a weekly basis via my newsletter. It's tailor-made for CEOs, executives and high-achievers like you.

Send an email to _kevin@lawrenceandco.com_ and put 'newsletter' in the subject line. Let me know where you're based and what industry you're in.

One Last Thought Before You Get Started

Yes, your development as a leader is serious business. But let yourself have fun as you work through the book. This is chance to learn about yourself, grow as a leader, and build an amazing life. Approach it with levity and an open mind. That'll take you far.

All the stories in this book are based on real-life people and situations but, in most cases, names have been changed for personal privacy.

~~~~~~~~~~~~~~ *STORY* ~~~~~~~~~~~~~~

When I first met Nigel, he was getting pummelled by life.

Although his business was seriously booming, he went to work every day with dread in the pit of his gut. Here was a guy who should have been plotting a huge, glorious future—but instead resisted the urge to vomit whenever he reached for his office door.

I talked Nigel out of his plan to ditch his company and run off to Tahiti, and we worked together to radically shift his mindset. His business—and his industry—had evolved over the years, and he hadn't kept up. He needed completely different tools to handle the intensity of life as a CEO.

So we met one morning a month to walk Vancouver's beautiful seawall (always good to get out of the office to get a fresh perspective), and talk through his issues. Ultimately, Nigel needed to deal with his emotional junk to manage his mental health, make more time for himself, teach his team to meet his standards, and make himself useless in his business. We put an action plan in place to deal with each of these issues head on, one by one.

Today, Nigel lives every business owner's fantasy. He sets the vision for his company, and has a partner who handles day-to-day operations. Much of Nigel's time is spent on personal passions—building homes for people in need, travelling with his family, and creating great experiences everywhere he goes.

Nigel is the perfect example of a leader who thought he needed to back down in order to survive success. He thought his booming business was too much for him, but there was never a need to succumb. He just needed a smarter way to push through.

Today his company is bigger than ever, and Nigel has reached an elusive state most leaders seek but never find: freedom.

You can read more about Nigel's story in his book, An Entrepreneur's Ride Through the Universe.

1

Live an Amazing Life

"Life is a great big canvas, and you should throw
all the paint on it you can."
DANNY KAYE, actor

Let me ask you this: Would you want someone you love to spend a lifetime living exactly as you are right now?

If your answer is not an enthusiastic, unqualified, 'Heck yeah', you've got work to do, my friend.

Life is meant to be a grand adventure. No one comes into this world only to have a booming business or legendary career. A truly great life is not just achievement...it's *enjoyment* of your achievement. It's enjoyment of life.

If you're not shouting from the mountaintops about your life, don't kid yourself into thinking you'll suddenly feel deep joy when your business reaches a certain pinnacle. That's not how life works.

It's easy to get addicted to success. Business achievement is a high that consumes many leaders—but it is not the *only* purpose in life.

You deserve, and can have, a much larger sense of fulfillment; a sense that all aspects of your life are rewarding and satisfying. As a leader, it's easy to lose sense of the bigger picture: to see nothing beyond hitting your next big goal.

Key Point
If you don't make time to enjoy what you achieve, your life might look great, but it won't feel great.

Too many successful people think they'll take better care of their health...later. They'll spend more time with their kids...later. They'll learn to sail...later.

Someday they'll do wildly generous things. *Someday* they'll finally enjoy everything they've achieved.

The problem is, you're already forming lifelong habits. The way you live right now is pretty much how you can expect to live in the future. Sure, you may have different possessions and assets, but you'll exist in a fundamentally similar way.

So if you're a 'maybe someday' sort of person, you're missing out. Stop delaying your life.

It is well within your power to enjoy every aspect of your life. You just need to make a clear decision to actually experience enjoyment, and stop procrastinating.

If you're like most leaders, you're used to planning for *achievement*—or what I like to call 'head success'. But this is only half of the equation. Head success is about reaching goals you set like revenue growth, profit, market share, personal wealth, possessions and vacations.

If you want a sense of satisfaction, you need to plan for *enjoyment* and *fulfillment*—aka 'heart success'. This requires defining how you want to feel about yourself and your life when you wake up every day.

Everyone has their own definition of heart success. You may want to feel energized, influential and connected to people you love. You may want to feel like you are making a profound difference in the world, and evolving as a human being.

However you define it, you need to sort out what heart success is to you so it can be part of your game plan.

If you play your cards right, you'll be able to look back, decades from now, with zero regrets. This is the true test of an amazing life.

Simple Summary

Success isn't *only* what you achieve or possess. It's how you *feel* about your life.

~~~~~~~~~~~~~~ *STORY* ~~~~~~~~~~~~~~

By the time he was 36, Robert had made more money than any other person in the history of his family. He built his business from the ground up, and it could reasonably be called an empire.

For much of his career, Robert had an unstoppable focus on work, with the goal of accumulating wealth and security for his loved ones.

Trouble is, all Robert knew how to do was make money, and save money. His financial position was ridiculously solid, but he couldn't bring himself to spend beyond the essentials—at all.

He dreamed of taking his family on vacations. He imagined buying pricey gifts for his kids. He longed for the day he would buy his hardworking, rough-and-tumble dad a new set of pipes for his Harley.

Robert had a generous heart, but he was so hard-wired to build wealth that, despite his best intentions, he couldn't part with his cash.

Finally the day came when his father's health faded, and it was clear he didn't have long to live. And it changed everything. Robert spent $5,000 to buy that set of exhaust pipes, and his dad's Harley never sounded louder, or felt more satisfying.

His dad rode that upgraded bike only once before he died, but the joy he experienced gave Robert a whole new take on money. He finally understood he needed to expand his definition of success.

His whole life he had seen success through one lens: his wealth goals. All decisions were based on maximizing his financial position. He learned to methodically weigh enjoyment of life as part of his decision-making criteria. This may sound simple and obvious, but for many driven people like Robert, it's a revelation.

Now, in addition to building wealth, Robert makes a concerted effort to create joy for himself and others. He bought the waterfront home he and his wife always wanted. He took his family on a trip around the world, and proudly owns a membership at a private track for car racing.

Sometimes that old perspective creeps up again, wanting Robert to pinch pennies and limit his enjoyment of life. When it does, he remembers his dad's Harley, and switches to a broader perspective.

Six Steps to Mastery

1. Figure out what makes your life amazing so far

We could sip a cappuccino and have a charming conversation about what's important to you, and what your ideal life would be. But this would be an intellectual exercise, generating only what's in your head.

Memories of your life's highlights are a sure-fire way to cut through the head success, and find out what heart success really is to you.

Action

Fill out the 1st column of Amazing Memories grid.

AMAZING MEMORIES GRID

AMAZING MEMORY	HEAD SUCCESS (ACHIEVEMENT) & WHY	HEART SUCCESS (ENJOYMENT) & WHY
1.		
2.		
3.		
4.		
5.		

2. Notice which successes mean the most

Sometimes success only strikes a chord with your head, not your heart. At other times you've probably managed to achieve both head and heart success simultaneously.

Action

Fill out the 2nd and 3rd columns on Amazing Memories grid. For each amazing memory note if it gave you a deep sense of enjoyment (heart success) or a sense of achievement (head success)—or both. Note why.

3. Discover what you would do if you had complete choice and freedom

Let your mind wander beyond the parameters of your current life by imagining the following scenario: You receive news that a long-lost relative has left you a $50 million inheritance. There are two strings attached:

- You must continue to work at least 30 hours a week, and be a contributing member of society.

- Your overall enjoyment of work and life must average at least eight out of 10, or the money vaporizes.

Action

What activities and pursuits would you start doing (or do more often)?
What activities and pursuits would you stop doing (or do less often)? Fill out the 1st row on the Amazing Life Grid.

AMAZING LIFE GRID

	START DOING (OR DO MORE) & WHY	STOP DOING (OR DO LESS) & WHY
$50 MILLION INHERITANCE		
12-YEAR-OLD WISDOM		
82-YEAR-OLD WISDOM		
GAME-OVER WISDOM		

4. Get advice from Young You, Old You and Game-Over You

12-Year-Old Wisdom: Imagine describing your life so far to a 12-year old version of yourself.

What changes would that child want you to make right now? Fill out the 2nd row on the Amazing Life Grid.

82-Year-Old Wisdom: Imagine describing your life so far to an 82-year old version of yourself.

What changes would that 82-year old want you to make right now? Fill out the 3rd row on the Amazing Life Grid.

Game-Over Wisdom: Nothing is quite as clarifying as mortality. If you knew this is your final year on this great planet, how you spend your days? What would you stop doing? Fill out the 4th row on the Amazing Life Grid.

5. Put it all together: Your Amazing Life Plan

Take what you've learned from the previous exercises. What themes or patterns do you notice?

_____

_____

_____

Action

Based on what you learned from the previous exercises, fill out the Amazing Life Plan. Choose your top three "achievement" _and_ top three "enjoyment" goals for the next 12 months.

Tip

Start with the 'Self' category.

AMAZING LIFE PLAN

	ACHIEVEMENT	ENJOYMENT
WORK		
SELF		
LIFE		

6. Build a better plan, and plan ahead – *well ahead*

An amazing life takes commitment and organization. You will only have a great life if you schedule things that make it great and stick to those commitments.

This is why my wife and I start each year knowing where we'll take our vacations. We make our bookings for the coming year in December, if not earlier.

Whatever your favourite activities are, start planning them. Book the concerts, brunches and dinner parties. Commit to your date nights. Schedule your volunteer time.

Of course, if you're the rare person who can be spontaneous with all your personal activities *and* run a booming business, my hat is off to you. But most of us need sound planning to make it happen.

Tip

Use birthdays and holidays to your advantage. These are great triggers for scheduling special events and get-togethers.

Action

What key things do you need to schedule for the coming 12 to 18 months?

1.
2.
3.
4.
5.

Tip

Think of your life as a massive R&D project. Keep experimenting, notice what works and what doesn't, and adjust at you go. An amazing life is an evolving life.

You Need to Work on This if...

1. You rate your current enjoyment of life less than nine out of 10.
2. You would feel you had used your life well, if it ended today.
3. You tend to use up your passion for work, and have little left for the rest of your life.
4. It's not normal for you to look forward to things in your life.
5. You often find yourself thinking or saying "woulda, coulda, shoulda".

Gut Check

Be brutally honest – how good are you at enjoying life in tandem with your head success?

On a scale of 0 (low) to 10 (high): _____

2

Forget Work-Life Balance

"You don't go to the amusement park roller coaster and say,
'I want to be balanced'. No, you want to be as unbalanced
as possible, because that's the thrill of the ride."
NEIL DEGRASSE TYSON, Astrophysicist

Work-life balance is a lovely notion. It may even work beautifully for people less ambitious than you. But it is _absolutely_ inconsistent with the life you've chosen, so you need to chuck it.

Balance is *not* for driven people.

You are fuelled to pursue wild, crazy, gigantic goals—and as wonderful as this is, it is not the making of a simple, balanced life.

You need to accept who you are. You're not a nine-to-fiver. If you live with the idea that you are supposed to have a balanced life as you chase huge goals, you'll always be tortured by feelings of guilt and inadequacy.

Work-self-life passion is about fully experiencing enthusiasm in all aspects of your life.

It is having the time and energy to:

- Fully enjoy _work_
- Have time just for your_self,_ and the things you most enjoy
- Have time for the people and personal causes you care about in _life._

Yes, it's possible. It first requires clear thinking about the distinct categories of your life:

Work: Everything you do professionally, including social events that are related to work, clients and colleagues.

Self: Things you do just for yourself because they replenish and make you stronger. If you don't invest energy in the 'self' category, you diminish your capacity to invest passion in work and life. Most leaders frequently and dangerously ignore this mission-critical category.

Life: These are the people and causes that matter to you most outside of work – including family, friends, charitable activities and the like. The time and energy spent here has nothing to do with furthering your business interests. It's about other things you love.

Invest Your Passion Units

So, think of it this way. If you have 100 units of passion to spend every week, you won't feel great if you spend 99 of them at work. This is a sure-fire route to misery. Your relationships would suffer tremendously. You would feel depleted. You would lose perspective on your life and your business, seriously limiting your ability to make clear, smart decisions.

Too many leaders use all of their energy and enthusiasm at the office, and then wonder why their relationships and personal satisfaction suffer.

Work-self-life passion requires you to consciously choose how you allot your passion units. It ensures you invest some in yourself, and those you love every week, allowing you to recharge.

If you make conscious choices about how you invest your passion, your experience of life can improve dramatically.

Simple Summary

Invest passion units in yourself first, to be as giving and productive as you want to be in other aspects of your life.

~~~~~~~~~~~ *INSIGHT* ~~~~~~~~~~~

I keep track of my work-self-life passion by noticing the parts of my life where I initiate new and interesting activities. It's my personality to spearhead new projects and plan great experiences, so for me this is a clear indicator.

I know I bring enough passion to my personal life when I use creative headspace to plan cool events for myself, and with friends and family. If I organize birthday parties, go-karting adventures, vacations, experiential activities, charitable events and the like, I'm investing a decent number of passion units outside of work.

When I have no energy left to plan personal experiences, it's a clear sign my passion units are off kilter.

~~~~~~

Four Steps to Mastery

1. Do a reality check

Where are your passion units currently expended? Said differently, where do you put your creative thinking and discretionary energy?

Be brutally honest. Are you only investing passion at work, and you and your family get the scraps left over at the end of the week? Are you, and the people you care about most, getting a decent measure of your creative headspace?

Action

Look back over the past month. What percentage of your best energy and creativity did you use for work, self and life? Or did you do nothing with it at all?

My Current Passion Ratio

Work % _____ Self % _____ Life % _____

2. Pick your ideal split

To be clear, I'm not saying your passion should be divided a third for work, a third for self, and a third for life. And in fact, this won't work unless you have a lifestyle business, or you've decided to kick back professionally.

For some leaders, greatness might be 60% work, 30% self, 10% life. For others it may be 65%, 20%, 15%.

Figure out the weighting that works for you. Ultimately it doesn't matter what you choose – just set a clear intention.

As a leader you will certainly go through brief periods where 90% of your passion is invested at work. This is unavoidable. Just understand it isn't sustainable, and you need to quickly get back to a healthier ratio.

Action

Choose your ideal Passion Ratio. Start with the 'self' category, or you may find only a small percentage of passion left for you.

My Ideal Passion Ratio

Work % _____ Self % _____ Life % _____

3. Choose differently

Knowing your Passion Ratio is only the start, of course. You then need to make different choices about where your energy and creativity are invested.

Action

What do you need to start – or stop doing – to align to
your Ideal Passion Ratio? Fill out the Passion Ratio Grid.

PASSION RATIO GRID

	WORK	SELF	LIFE
CURRENT PASSION RATIO			
IDEAL PASSION RATIO			
START OR DO MORE OFTEN			
STOP OR DO LESS OFTEN			

4. Keep tweaking

Having energy and passion for all aspects of your life is
a journey. Your Passion Ratio isn't a change you make
once in your life, and never think about again.

It requires constant reflection. Are you living your ratio?
How does it feel? What needs to change?

Action

Make sure you reflect on your Passion Ratio every time you do your annual and quarterly planning. Always do this in writing, noting your observations, and the tweaks that need to happen.

You Need to Work on This if...

1. Your life feels out of control, or you feel guilty about not having 'work-life balance'.
2. Life doesn't feel like you thought it would at your level of success.
3. You don't enjoy life outside of work as much as you'd like.
4. You rarely or never take time just for yourself. Or if you do, you feel guilty about it.
5. You've lost touch with people and causes outside of work you care about.

Gut Check

How adept are you at finding time and energy for all aspects of your life?

On a scale of 0 (low) to 10 (high): _____

3

Double Your Resilience

"A good half of the art of living is resilience."
ALAIN DE BOTTON, Swiss-born British author

You don't expect a thoroughbred racehorse to perform at its peak without proper care, so why expect this of yourself?

Yes, you are the kind of person who loves to push your limits, and take on big challenges. You have more drive, stamina and sheer willpower than most people dream of.

But you still need care and attention to perform at your best, or you will definitely crash and burn.

Whenever I see a leader collapse under the weight of responsibility and success, I know the collapse was both predictable and preventable.

Somewhere along the line that leader stopped doing the things that keep him or her healthy because life got busy. That leader dropped personal well-being to the bottom of the priority list.

With the huge, adventurous life you've chosen, your well-being must come first for you to have the strength to keep going and keep giving. You need to continually replenish your oxygen, your energy and your stamina.

Don't leave this to chance. You need a system for making sure you take care of yourself, even when there are a billion other urgent priorities.

Let me introduce you to the 'Resilience Rituals'. Your Resilience Rituals are your very own, unique combination of body, mind and spirit activities that put you at your very best.

> **Key Point**
> When you stay true to your Resilience Rituals, you set yourself up to win, no matter what life throws at you.

Your Resilience Rituals include three essential elements:

1. Things you do to take care of your **body**: going to the gym, yoga, trail running, soccer – whatever works for you.

2. Things you do to take care of your **mind**: activities that help you mentally re-centre. Journaling and meditation are your best options.

3. Things you do to take care of your **spirit**: activities that light you up inside more than anything else. They give you a sense that all your hard work is worth it; that your life has meaning. Only you can know what these are for you, and they may be anything.

Maybe your Resilience Rituals are karate, meditation and sunset walks with your spouse. Or maybe your combo is yoga, journaling and sailing the high seas.

When you commit to your Resilience Rituals, you breathe more deeply. Your worries are quieter. Your mind is at its sharpest. Your creativity is at its peak. And you rebound faster from setbacks.

Hear this: you *cannot* cheat and say, 'Oh running helps me in all three categories, so I'll just run.' Nope. That's a fail, for sure. At your elite level of performance, you need activities that specifically support you in each category.

The key is to know your Resilience Rituals and do them *all the time*. Make them a non-negotiable part of your normal routine, no matter what's happening at work or home.

Sound like a big commitment? Is breathing a big commitment? Your Resilience Rituals are life giving. Energy giving. They create time and space. So do them.

Simple Summary

When your strength and resilience are a priority, you'll have the stamina to give even more.

―――――〜〜〜――――― *STORY* ―――――〜〜〜―――――

I learned the hard lesson of self-sustainability early in life.

I crashed and burned dramatically in the very first year, of my very first post-college job.

At the ripe age of 23, I placed first *and second* in our annual sales competition, winning a three-week trip to Europe. I did so while sitting on two volunteer boards, running several record-setting charity fundraisers, and generally wreaking havoc every weekend as a typical 20-something.

Everyone was in awe. My boss wanted to clone me.

But 12 months in I hit the wall. Hard. It took me more than a year to recover.

For driven people, our greatest strength is also our greatest downfall. Yes, ambition and capacity lead to cash and accolades. But it also makes us blind to our personal needs. It causes us to drive right off a cliff, and wonder how the heck that happened.

On the upside, I was forced to learn a lot about managing the intensity of life. As a result, my career as a coach was born (though my lessons about burnout were only beginning).

Whether you've hit the wall already in your life or not, you need to accept that human beings require care. You are not some magical exception.

Your body, mind and spirit need recharging. Constantly.

ADD and ADHD are incredibly common among leaders of high-growth companies.

And it's no wonder. People with these conditions have attributes well suited to leadership.

The gifts of ADD/ADHD are tons of energy and creativity, and a massive amount of drive. This unstoppable drive also means an even bigger risk than most of crashing and burning – self care is even more critical.

If you're someone with ADD or ADHD, your Resilience Rituals are not to be taken lightly. They are critical to keep you in a balanced, healthy state.

Five Steps to Mastery

1. Know your history

Think about the periods in your life when you felt fantastic and amazingly strong. I don't mean individual moments – I mean ongoing periods of time when you felt inspired, buoyant and invincible. What were you doing to take care of your body, mind and spirit?

Action

Fill out the When I Felt Strongest Grid.

WHEN I FELT STRONGEST GRID

TIME PERIOD	1.	2.	3.
BODY: HOW DID I KEEP MY BODY FEELING ENERGIZED AND/OR STRONG?			
MIND: HOW DID I KEEP MY MIND CLEAR AND/OR FOCUSED?			
SPIRIT: WHAT DID I FIND REWARDING AND/OR INSPIRING?			

2. Deepen your understanding

All three aspects of your Resilience Rituals (body, mind and spirit) are mission critical and interdependent. It's crucial to understand the importance of each one.

Body

A healthy sleep pattern and good nutrition are absolutely fundamental to your physical strength and resilience. But these alone are not nearly enough.

Most leaders spend hours on end sitting in a chair. It's essential to make some form of exercise a major priority to counteract this.

Exercise isn't just about fitness or physical health. It is a crucial way to release stress, change your perspective, and get endorphins surging through your body. You are pretty much guaranteed to feel better when you're active. Now, some people can decide to workout regularly, and do it without fail. Others need structure and support to make it happen.

Many of my clients have trainers for this purpose. A scheduled commitment to a trainer makes sticking to your workouts far easier. A good trainer will push you harder than you would push yourself.

Ultimately, there's no right way to be active. For you, it may be yoga or dance classes. For someone else, it may be a team sport, kickboxing, cycling or swimming.

What matters is that you choose something you enjoy, and that it is a non-negotiable part of your schedule, at least two or three times a week.

Mind

You need a way to calm your active mind, and take control of it. It is meant to support you, not drive you crazy. I can tell you after years of experimentation, there are two options I recommend above all others: journaling and meditation. But if you have another practice that clears and re-centers your mind, by all means go for it.

If I'm feeling anxious, stressed or unclear about something, journaling puts me in a completely new headspace. I can go from frenzied to relaxed, or confused to clear, in 15 minutes flat.

I pour all of the seemingly random thoughts bouncing around in my brain onto the page. Pen to paper works magic every single time.

For others, a consistent meditation practice offers the same benefit. But whatever method you choose, you can't be haphazard about it. It can't be a last resort; it needs to be a steady part of your life.

It's absolutely crucial to understand that *you can't use distraction or denial to manage stress over the long term*. Your worried thoughts must somehow be evacuated from your brain, or they will keep recycling endlessly. No matter how you do it, you need to make your mind a tool that you control and direct.

So yes, you may have a calmer mind after your daily run or spin class, and this is helpful, but it is not the same as managing your mind. To be at your best, you need both physical and mental supports.

Spirit

Last, but definitely not least, you need to know what makes your spirit strong.

The best way I can describe this is to say that these are activities that feed you in a way that other things in life do not: things you do simply for the joy of it. Things that light you up inside. Things outside work that inspire and reward you.

Some people need time alone in nature, or quiet contemplation, relaxing on the back porch. Others may have a particular passion for learning about history or philosophy. For you it may be painting, sketching, volunteering, gardening, car racing or climbing the world's tallest peaks.

Action

Fill out the Resilience Ritual Brainstorming grid.

RESILIENCE RITUAL BRAINSTORMING GRID

BODY: WHAT MAKES YOU FEEL PHYSICALLY AT YOUR BEST?	
MIND: WHAT HELPS YOU CLEAR YOUR HEAD AND GET FOCUSED?	
SPIRIT: WHAT ACTIVITIES LIGHT YOU UP INSIDE?	

3. Draft your Resilience Rituals

Reflect on what you wrote in exercises #1 and #2, as well as anything else you know about what makes you feel strong and vibrant.

Based on your insights, create a first draft of your Resilience Rituals.

I've included mine below as an example. If you need more sources of inspiration, notice what's working for people around you. It can also be useful to read articles or biographies about the personal habits of successful people.

Action

Fill out the first two columns (What & Frequency) on the My Resilience Rituals Grid.

MY RESILIENCE RITUALS GRID

	WHAT	FREQUENCY	WHEN
BODY	• •		
MIND	• •		
SPIRIT	• •		

KEVIN'S RESILIENCE RITUALS GRID

	WHAT	FREQUENCY	WHEN
BODY	• Workout with trainer • Other activities: Walk, bike or hike	3× a week 3× a week	6am 6am or on weekends
MIND	• Journal for 10 -15 minutes • Update my to-do lists	3× a week 5× a week	7am (after workout) 8:00am (weekdays)
SPIRIT	• Adventures with loved ones • Push my limits with like-minded people (e.g. motorsports)	2× a month 1 to 2× a month	Weekends, evenings Weekends

4. Commit to your Resilience Rituals – even when they anger or annoy others

You must make it a priority to take care of yourself, and do your Resilience Rituals religiously. Remember, you have to stay strong to give as much as you do to other people, and the world.

A simple way to stick to your commitment is to do the daily aspects of your rituals first thing every morning. Deepak Chopra, best-selling author and spiritual teacher, claims his early mornings for himself. He starts each day at 4am to meditate and write until 9am. Then he's available to others for the rest of the day.

However you choose to structure your Resilience Rituals, the most crucial thing is to schedule them, and stick to them.

Action

When will you do each of your Resilience Rituals activities? Fill in the 'When' category on the Resilience Rituals Grid.

5. Adjust your Resilience Rituals as needed

Your Resilience Rituals are meant to evolve, as you learn more about yourself, and as your interests change over time. You need to closely observe the way you feel overall, to know if your rituals work for you, if tweaks are needed, or if you've outgrown certain activities.

Notice your levels of inspiration and energy. Notice your patience and stress levels. Notice what activities work for you.

You may need to shake things up now and again. If you decide to stop an activity in the physical category, replace it with another physical activity. The same applies to your mind and spirit activities; otherwise your rituals will lose their effect.

Only you can know when your rituals are really humming. Invest the time to experiment and fine-tune your formula.

Action

Keep looking for other ways to improve your Resilience Rituals. Test to see if you notice an improvement or not.

You Need to Work on This if...

1. You continually run out of energy, feel tired or get sick.
2. You are not enjoying the challenges, or the wins, at work or in life.
3. You regularly allow other people's priorities to bump the activities you want to do for your own wellness.
4. You've stopped doing the activities that bring you a feeling of reward and inspiration. Maybe you don't even know what they are anymore.
5. You feel a need to escape from your work or life.

Gut Check

How well are you currently maintaining your personal resilience?
On a scale of 0 (low) to 10 (high): _____

4

Invest In Your Sweet Spots

*"Success is achieved by developing our strengths,
not by eliminating our weaknesses."*
MARILYN VON SAVANT, highest recorded IQ
in the Guinness Book of Records

Your sweet spot is an actual thing, not just an abstract idea.

It's doing the things you love to do the way you love to do them.

It also happens to be where you deliver by far the most value. Your sweet spot talents are so indisputable it is criminal to waste your energy elsewhere. This is where you have vitality and inspiration, oxygen coursing through your system.

Unfortunately, conventional wisdom leads you to believe you're supposed to care about improving your weaknesses. This is nonsense. It's a path that leads to mediocrity. And ultimately, it's a sure-fire recipe for disaster, physically and mentally. It drains your oxygen supply, depleting your energy, creativity and enthusiasm for life.

DO NOT get suckered into thinking work isn't supposed to be fun or easy. It's not your job to fit some Holy Grail, universal model of leadership. Such a thing doesn't exist anyway.

There are dozens of ways to be a great leader. You need to figure out _your_ way. Let go of the stuff that simply isn't your strong suit or passion.

If you're good with numbers, but your brain bleeds with boredom at the mention of accounting, stop torturing yourself. Accept that accounting isn't your sweet spot –and make sure someone on your team has both the passion and aptitude for it.

Key Point
Spend 80% of your time and energy doing things you love to do, the way you love to do them.

First things first: Figure out your true sweet spot. This is harder than it seems because, let's face it, you've acquired a vast set of skills to get to where you are today. It's easy to confuse what you _can_ do, with what you _love_ to do.

Simple Summary
Stop boring yourself or torturing yourself with tasks outside your sweet spot. You deliver the most value doing what you love.

Nicole is the kind of executive you trust with your biggest, craziest projects. She figures things out when everyone else throws up their hands in frustration. If it's wild and ambitious, or difficult and seemingly unsolvable, Nicole is your go-to person.

Despite her long history of strategizing and launching successful projects, Nicole kept getting the same unpleasant feedback in performance reviews. She was celebrated for her heroism at the launch phase, but criticized for her inability to be a solid day-to-day manager, once her projects were operational.

Year after year she tried to hone her managerial skills, attempting to morph into the type of executive who deftly oversees an established program. But boredom overtook, and she'd find herself distracted by the prospect of a brand new challenge.

She'd think something was wrong with her, believing she must lack ability or strategic thinking. The guilt dragged her down at work – and at home.

Working with Nicole, it was instantly clear to me that launching crazy projects is, in fact, her sweet spot. That's how she delivers tremendous value. She is simply not the person to put on day-to-day management tasks.

It's a waste of her talent, and those responsibilities are best left to someone else.

Nicole had a heart-to-heart with her CEO, and is now officially the exec for special projects. It's all she does and, because of this, the company has pulled off some unbelievable feats.

She had to let go of the idea that she could morph into a different kind of leader, and turn some beloved projects over to people who have the right personality and skills to manage them day-to-day. But the net result is, she's never been more successful or satisfied.

Six Steps to Mastery

1. Examine your patterns of success to understand your natural ability.

Success leaves clues. Your sweet spot is similar throughout your life. The reason you were class valedictorian, or a track star, is probably similar to the reason your first company was a smashing success.

Action

Take a look at your track record, and fill out the first two columns on the Historical Sweet Spots Grid. Make a list of your top five achievements to date, in work and life. For each one, note what natural ability made you succeed.

HISTORICAL SWEET SPOTS GRID

ACHIEVEMENT	NATURAL ABILITY	ENVIRONMENT
1.		
2.		
3.		
4.		
5.		

2. Know your ideal environment

Your performance is significantly affected by circumstances and environment. You will get different results doing the same task in different situations.

Some people do their best creative thinking alone at home. Some need to be out in nature. Others are best in group settings.

You may power through a pile of tasks best when your favourite music is pumping. Or you may like to silence every device, and let stillness ring through your workspace.

Tight deadlines might motivate you, or you might work better without any pressure or urgency.

Action

Pinpoint the environmental factors that matter to you by looking again at your top five achievements on the Historical Sweet Spots Grid. Fill out the 3rd column, noting the defining features of the environment. Some things to consider:

- Was it a team environment or an individual situation?
- If it was a team, was it a new team or one with a long history?
- Were you under a lot of pressure or not?
- Was there an urgent deadline or not?
- Was there a creative aspect to your role?
- Did you create something brand new, or improve something that already existed?
- Was it a global project? Local?

3. Notice what you love about your work (past and present)

It helps to notice the things you gravitate to first in your workday. What tasks do you tend to do first in your current role? In past roles?

In my case, I gravitate to any task that involves interacting with driven people who have high-stakes problems to solve. If I have a list of documents to review, and a bunch of phone calls to make, I'll always pick up the phone first. That's what I love. Helping driven people gives me energy.

Action

Fill out the 'Love To Do' list.

LOVE TO DO LIST

WHAT ENERGIZES ME WHAT I LOVE TO DO	WHAT DRAINS ME WHAT I AVOID
1.	
2.	
3.	
4.	

4. Draft Your Sweet Spot

Based on everything you learned from the exercises above, what do you love to do and how do you love to do it?

Action

Articulate your sweet spot.

My Sweet Spot

What I love to do, and do well:

_____

_____

How I love to do it (i.e. the environment):

_____

_____

5. Move toward spending 80% of your time in your sweet spot

You perform at your best if you spend 80% of your time in your sweet spot. For most people, getting there is a journey that involves letting go of personal responsibility for tasks outside the sweet spot.

You also need to start consciously creating situations that put you at your best. So if you know you need quiet time alone to do your best thinking, what's your plan for securing that time? If you're at your best in a high-energy group setting with big, urgent deadlines, how do you create that?

Action

Do an honest assessment of your current situation. How much time do you currently spend in your sweet spot, doing work you love, and how you love doing it?

Sweet Spot Reality Check

Current % of time: _____%

Goal for next six months: _____%

6. Making the shift

How will you move more toward spending 80% of your time in your sweet spot? List three things you need to start doing (or do more often), and three things you need to stop doing (or do less often).

What do you need to start doing (or do more often)?

1.
2.
3.

What do you need to stop doing (or do less often)?

1.	
2.	
3.	

Tip

Self-assessments can really help you zero in on your sweet spot. They give you a model for understanding your natural strengths. My favourites are *DiSC* and *Strengths*. Both are reasonably inexpensive, quick and painless, and give valuable insight you can apply immediately.

You Need to Work on This if...

1. Most of your days feel like a struggle because you're doing a slew of stuff you don't enjoy.
2. You don't feel inspired to do the work that's on your to-do list.
3. There are important, high-value tasks you intend to do every week that never get done.
4. There are aspects of your work that are mediocre, but you don't have the energy or desire to improve them.
5. You generally feel blah, or drained at the end of day.

Gut Check

How good are you at spending the vast majority of your time and energy in your sweet spot?

On a scale of 0 (low) to 10 (high): _____

5

Lick Your Toads

"You may delay, but time will not."
BENJAMIN FRANKLIN

You know those annoying tasks you procrastinate because there are more important things to focus on?

Yeah, all those nasty, irritating to-do's accumulating into big piles of awfulness that drain your life-force.

I'm referring to tasks like taking your car in for repair, upgrading the data plan for your phone, transcribing the notes you took at a conference, fixing a squeaky door, returning a call you'd rather ignore, completing your will...you get the idea.

I call these irritating tasks 'toads', because they are the kind of thing that make you recoil. You'd rather not touch them, or even think about them, if you don't have to.

Key Point
Get your toads done so your energy is
freed up for bigger and better things.

Here's what I mean: if at some point this year, you absolutely *had* to lick a slimy, fly-infested toad all the way from its bumpy head, to the base of its icky back, when would you schedule that lovely task? You'd probably wait until the very end of the year rather than getting it over with immediately.

That's human nature.

But that nasty task would weigh on your mind all year, even when you weren't aware of it. Instead of fully focusing on the important things in life, you'd expend energy dreading and procrastinating that unpleasant task.

You know what would happen if you just went ahead and did the deed? You'd freak out very briefly, and then breathe a sigh of relief, and tell me, 'Ok, that wasn't so bad. I'm relieved it's over.'

When it comes to life's annoyances, dreading is always worse than doing. *Always.* When you get rid of them you float freer in life.

Yet most people go through life with 150 seemingly benign to-dos at any given time. I'm going to guess you're saying to yourself, 'Not me – I don't have 150 annoyances kicking around.' But if we sat down together and made a list, your head would spin at how fast you'd reach 150.

Why? *Because you keep accumulating them.* You think adding one more item to the semi-conscious list at the back of your mind expends less energy than just doing the thing. On this point you are drastically mistaken.

You don't notice how these tasks drag you down; how they accompany you in every moment of your day.

The only way to free yourself is to stop procrastinating. Get into the habit of licking your nastiest toad first thing each morning, to start the day free and strong.

Simple Summary

The little things you procrastinate consume far more energy than you believe. Get them out of the way.

———————— *STORY* ————————

Bashir is a remarkable executive, and one of the worst procrastinators I've ever met in my life.

He's incredibly smart, and I'm sure if we ran an IQ test, he'd be in the Mensa range. But as a leader his growth was stunted. He couldn't advance because he spent his days trying to catch up on his workload. Guilt piled as high as the tasks, and gnawed at the pit of his stomach until he literally became ill.

The reality was that Bashir had the potential to improve, but he didn't know how to do it.

When we started working together, he had well over 150 different items dragging him down. As we cleaned up all the issues, one by one, he had more and more bandwidth to put toward strategic work.

Now that I've worked with him for several years, I can tell as soon as I hear his voice if his toads are out of control. If he has less than 10, he sounds like his normal, everyday self – warm, clear-headed, and smart.

LICK YOUR TOADS | 71

If he lets his list accumulate to 15 or more, look out. He's distracted, uncertain, and wild with stress.

Our very first agenda item, every time we meet, is to review his Toad's List—and we make sure to refresh it quarterly.

Today, with a system in place, he's much better at staying on top of it—especially now that he understands the obvious correlation to his mental well-being, and his growth and progress as a leader.

~~~~~~

25 Common Toads

1. Giving feedback to underperforming employees
2. Changing roles for employees
3. Firing or demoting employees
4. Saying no
5. Dealing with unresolved conflicts
6. Asking customers for feedback
7. Calling customers for money
8. Firing bad clients
9. Thanking customers
10. Telling a client you made a mistake
11. Tolerating late or incorrect orders
12. Closing or selling a business, or part of a business
13. Ending or renegotiating a joint venture
14. Booking vacations and taking time to recharge
15. Scheduling doctors appointments

16. Spending quality time with loved ones
17. Making decisions related to family, home and finances
18. Unresolved conflicts or arguments
19. Finding a therapist
20. Planning for retirement
21. Doing your taxes
22. Doing your will
23. Dealing with clutter at home
24. Handling home repairs
25. Working on personal relationships.

Five Steps to Mastery

1. Know your toads

Unlock the toads from the recesses of your mind. Dig 'em out. Write 'em down. Make a list of every single one, large and small.

Think of this as mental spring cleaning, excavating the irritants from your mind.

Include every to-do that gives you an unpleasant twinge when it pops into your head. Just getting these down on paper is an achievement, because it will spur you to take action.

Action

Write down the first 30 toads that come to your mind. Use the '25 Common Toads' list as a prompt.

30 TOADS

1.
2.
3.
4.
5.
6.
7.
8.
9.
10.
11.
12.
13.
14.
15.
16.
17.
18.
10.
20.
21.
22.
23.
24.
25.
26.
27.
28.
29.
30.

2. Lick 10 toads in 10 days

This is the best way to train yourself to make toad-licking a habit.

Action

Pick 10 toads from your 30 Toads list to complete within a 10-day period. Write them on the 1st column of the My First 10 Toads Grid. They can be large or small. It doesn't matter. This is about reducing your backlog to free up your energy, and create a habit of regularly handling annoyances.

As your backlog diminishes, you'll notice more spring in your step, and be encouraged to keep the process going. At the end of your 10-day period, note your increased energy level. Note what it feels like to have fewer worries in your mind. Yes, licking toads is briefly unpleasant, but the payback is major.

Tip

You might like to pick easy toads to kick-start some momentum. Or you might want to tackle some tough ones that really drag you down. Or a combo. Do what motivates you most.

MY FIRST 10 TOADS GRID

TOAD	THE "D" TO USE
1.	
2.	
3	
4.	
5.	
6.	
7.	
8.	
9.	
10	

3. Employ the Five D's

There's more than one way to lick a toad. It's not always appropriate for you to personally handle it. Sometimes it's not yours to do at all. Sometimes you know it'll never happen if it stays in your court.

There are five standard ways to tackle annoyances. For each toad on your list, review the options below, and choose the one that makes the most sense for the situation:

1. **Do it.** Bite the bullet immediately.

2. **Don't do it**. Say 'no' to the person who requested it, if it's simply not yours to do.

3. **Delegate it**. Assign an appropriate person.

4. **Delete it**. Let go of it entirely. Decide it's not going to happen.

5. **Date it**. Commit to completing it by a specific date sometime down the road. _Do not_ use this as a default. Only apply this when now is truly not the right time to deal with the task.

Action
Refer back to the My First 10 Toads Grid. For each toad, note which of the Five D's you will use.

4. Lick your nastiest toad first thing every morning

Congrats. You have a new life habit.

Handling your nastiest toad every morning is the single most effective way to free up your energy, and to end procrastination.

Before you've checked email or sipped caffeine, lick your nastiest toad. Then notice the difference in how your day unfolds. You will inevitably feel more empowered, more energized, and more enthusiastic about the day ahead. You've conquered a toad, and it's barely dawn. You are already heroic.

Also, notice the difference when you don't muster the fortitude to lick that toad. The stress of it will linger with you throughout your day, pestering you. Distracting you. Dragging you down.

I ask my clients to wake up every day knowing the three most important things they need to get done that day. Number 1 must be their biggest toad (the thing they least want to do). I view this as a mastery-level leadership habit.

TODAY'S TOP THREE TOADS:

1.
2.
3.

Action

Make a top three list to complete before you start your day tomorrow.

5. Schedule a Toad Day at the office

This is so much more fruitful than Casual Day.

Make toad-licking part of your corporate culture. Schedule an afternoon (once a quarter or twice a year) that is exclusively about getting annoying tasks completed. Ask each of your team members to create a list of 30 work and personal toads. On Toad Day, challenge everyone to see how many they can complete.

This is a sure-fire way to revitalize your team, and to get creative energy flowing again. People perform far better without a backlog of toads dragging them down.

Toad Day is a powerful statement about the kind of culture you are fostering. It asks people to push through obstacles, and just do what needs doing.

Action

Pick a potential date for your first team Toad Day.

_____

Tip

You can call Toad Day whatever you want, of course –
Spring Cleaning Day, Fresh Start Day, Catch Up Day.
Whatever fits your corporate culture.

You Need to Work On This if...

1. Reading this chapter makes you tense.
2. It's not unusual for to-dos to kick around for a month
   or more.
3. Certain lingering to-dos cause you frustration or anxiety.
4. People repeatedly ask you to follow through on certain tasks.
5. People are noticeably annoyed at your lack of follow through.

Gut Check

How do you rate at getting annoying things done before they
pile up?
On a scale of 0 (low) to 10 (high): _____

6

Deal With Your Emotional Junk

"We are enslaved by anything we do
not consciously see. We are freed by
conscious perception."

VERNON HOWARD, author, spiritual teacher, philosopher

You need to freely make the decisions you really want to make, even when it ruffles feathers, damages egos, or causes a minor earthquake within your company.

This takes nerves of steel. At times, if you're like most leaders, it's hard to be that bold.

That's because sometimes your emotional junk (residue from challenging times in your life) is right at the surface, diminishing your ability to do what needs to be done. This residue often takes the form of unconscious thoughts.

It may cause you to question yourself, worry what other people think, or behave in ways you later regret.

Past traumas leave emotional junk in your brain, invisibly, subconsciously affecting your behaviour and decisions. This junk lowers your emotional intelligence, weakening your true capacity as a leader. It elicits strong emotions, and diminishes your ability to think strategically. It compromises your integrity, and can stop you from saying or doing what needs to be done.

Key Point
Get rid of your emotional junk so it doesn't cause bad decisions or regrettable behaviour.

Most leaders limit their freedom by ignoring or denying their emotional junk. But it's still there, affecting you whether or not you're comfortable acknowledging it. And if you don't clean it up, you can never be truly free no matter how much money or success you have.

Of course no one likes to admit they have emotional junk. But these battle wounds are a fact of life for everyone; a universal fact of the human experience.

If you don't clean up your wounds, they can flare up at inconvenient times, causing your mind to switch to survival mode.

They can make you act like a fool, which, needless to say, is bad for business.

You need to be able to respond intelligently in every situation instead of reacting emotionally.

Simple Summary
Don't let emotional junk hold you back as a leader.

Phil was having a hard time scaling his company.

Despite a team of well-paid execs, he often seemed to be doing everything himself. He was run ragged, continuously exhausted and frustrated. The company was doing well enough, but not growing at the pace he knew it could.

Phil is the sort of character who is uncomfortable around people. Afraid to give feedback, and to push people to actually do their jobs well, he would go to the ends of the earth to prevent them from leaving. That included doing their jobs for them – making him so busy even the thought of looking for another key person made him want to explode.

Worse still, every few months or so, when a member of his executive team decided to quit, Phil panicked and threw more cash at the person to prevent a departure.

His underperforming team cost him more and more money. And he didn't understand his execs were totally playing him.

As I started to work with Phil, he realized that he tolerated bad behaviour and mediocre performance because of his own issues. He became motivated to make big changes in himself, and his company.

First he needed to work with a therapist to deal with the emotional junk from his childhood that made him uncomfortable around people.

Then he replaced his exec team with personality types that are a better fit for him, and with people sincerely committed to their jobs.

He hired a human resources expert to help him clearly articulate his expectations of the executives, and to teach him how to give better feedback.

And as a workaround, he uses me to help him handle some of the tougher interpersonal issues, keeping everyone in line.

With the right tools, and the right support, Phil's company is now growing at an impressive clip. Personally he is stronger by the month, and professionally he's growing as a leader.

~~~~~~

Five Steps to Mastery

1. If you're emotional, don't decide or react
This simple rule of leadership must never be broken. Emotions are wonderful, but they are destructive and misleading when it comes to decision-making.

Whether it's anger, frustration, sadness, excitement – or any other emotion – let it settle before you make a decision or react to a situation.

When the emotion has settled, you see things more clearly. You communicate more neutrally. You hear more accurately.

You are far less likely to regret something you say or do. Your decisions are more sound and strategic.

Action

Next time you're feeling emotional about a decision or something you're about to do, wait 24 hours, and let the emotion subside.

2. Know your emotional junk

You can uncover your emotional junk by noticing the kinds of situations that make you tense. Notice when you seek other people's approval, or act in a way that is out of character. Notice when you back down from what you really want.

Maybe you have a hard time saying 'no' to people who admire you. Or you retreat when people get upset. Maybe you have a weakness for charming but mediocre people. Or you explode when you see someone being taken advantage of.

Whatever your triggers are, when they are activated, they affect your thinking and decision-making.

Action

Use the Emotional Junk Grid to track what causes your bad decisions, or regrettable behaviour. Fill out the first two columns of the grid.

EMOTIONAL JUNK GRID EXAMPLE

BAD DECISION OR REGRETTABLE BEHAVIOUR	EMOTIONAL JUNK	WORKAROUND
1. Waited to fire employee.	Uncomfortable with conflict	Get HR involved early
2. Hired the wrong ad agency	Pressured by marketing VP	Express opinion in writing when pressured
3. Unsafe driving to meeting	Worry clients will lose respect	Leave 15 minutes earlier than you think you need to
4. Yelled at employee	Triggered by disrespect	End conversations as soon as anger arises

EMOTIONAL JUNK GRID

BAD DECISION OR REGRETTABLE BEHAVIOUR	EMOTIONAL JUNK	WORKAROUND
1.		
2.		
3.		
4.		

3. Have workarounds

When you know your emotional junk, you can have workarounds in place to keep yourself in check. You can find an alternate path to take for each of your emotional triggers.

Workarounds can be as simple as seeking a second opinion, waiting 24 hours before you act, saying no, not making decisions when you are tired, requiring someone else to be a part of specific meetings or decisions, or not emailing when you are mad.

In my case, I leave really early for all client meetings and flights so I'm not triggered by lateness. I request follow-up conversations when my anger arises, to prevent blasting people in the heat of the moment.

Action

Fill out the 'Workaround' column on the Emotional Junk Grid.

4. Know the warning signs

Let's be honest. You know when you're about to say something stupid, or make a bad decision. You can feel it happening. You know when you're in *that* mode.

Now you need to learn to interrupt yourself <u>before</u> you do or say something regrettable. This is simply a matter of increasing your awareness.

At first, you may only be slightly aware as the thing is happening, but then acutely aware afterward. For example, you may feel frustration rising, and yell at someone even though there's a part of you that really doesn't want to do it.

With concerted attention, you can become aware fast enough to intervene; to turn the situation around as it's happening. So you might say something like, 'Wow, I'm feeling angry about this. I take back what I just said. Let's talk about this again tomorrow when I'm calmer."

Eventually – and this is the Holy Grail – you'll be able to predict well in advance that certain types of situations are likely to trigger you. Then you can take action before you're triggered. Bad behaviour and bad decisions need not happen.

It all begins by noticing when you're going into *that* mode. I get a sensation in my chest when I'm about to say something harsh. Some people feel backed into a corner right before they make a bad decision. Others have a panicky sensation.

Action

What physical or emotional sensations are warning signs that you're getting triggered to behave badly, or make a regrettable decision?

1.	
2.	
3.	
4.	
5.	

5. Clean up the junk

Workarounds help to get you through tricky situations, but they can't eliminate the underlying emotional junk. You can clean up small bits of junk working with a coach, but bigger, tougher issues require a psychologist.

When you roll up your sleeves to clean up your triggers, you learn fascinating stuff. You may discover that the reason you freak out so easily about money is that your parents went bankrupt when you were 11, and you never really processed the stress of that event.

You may discover the reason you're so quickly triggered by aggressive personalities is that you were bullied in grade three, or that you were a bully in grade three.

Maybe your parents were immigrants so you always feel the need to prove your worth at any cost. Or you were harshly reprimanded for being anything less than top of your class.

Everyone has some sort of emotional junk to clean up. It's part of being human.

Does it sound annoying or time-consuming to surface and process this stuff? It doesn't have to be.

But it does require willingness. It's important to realize your choice to deal with your emotional junk is ultimately what determines how far you can go as a leader. More leaders are foiled by emotional junk than any other cause.

With the right professional, you can clear the junk from your system efficiently. The improvements in your abilities as a leader will be significant and fast.

Action

Which professional(s) could help you clean up your emotional junk? Contact one this week to get the ball rolling.

1.	
2.	

～～ KEVIN'S SPEED-SHOPPING ～～ WORKAROUND

I have an unfortunate history of shopping in a mad rush, and later questioning my sanity. This is directly caused by my time-scarcity problem, and compounded by my drive to get things done.

So I created a personal rule. I only make a purchase if my gut clearly says, 'Heck, yeah.'

When I'm not sure about a purchase, I tell the salesperson I'll come back in an hour or so if I still want it. I may ask them to hold it for the rest of the day.

If it's an online purchase, I leave the item in the cart for a day or two.

I find whenever I give myself space and time, I quickly realize the item really is – or isn't – for me.

You Need to Work on This if...

1. You sometimes back down from decisions you really want to make.

2. What others will think of you factors too heavily into your decisions.

3. You are sometimes shocked or embarrassed by your own behaviour.

4. Your emotional reactions are sometimes disproportionate to the issue at hand.

Gut Check

How good are you at not responding irrationally or emotionally? On a scale of 0 (low) to 10 (high): _____

7

Manage Your Mental Health

*"It's not the heavy load that breaks you down. It's
the way you carry it."*
LENA HORNE, Jazz Icon & Civil Rights Activist

Mental health is the big secret of the boardroom.

You're in good company if, at times, you suffer mentally and emotionally. No one is immune, not even the hardiest among us.

And is it any wonder? Leaders constantly face the harsh realities of business, and the curveballs of life. This puts you at higher risk for a mental health crisis, and makes managing mental wellness a must-have skill.

The uneasy truth is you can handle stress until you can't.

A mental health crisis is a freak storm. It may arise as depression, anxiety, mental exhaustion, uncontrollable stress, panic attacks, severe anger, social withdrawal, substance abuse or an eating disorder (to name a few possibilities).

It happens when stress outpaces your tried-and-true coping mechanisms, your energy gets depleted; your oxygen supply is drained. In these dark moments, the only rational step is to find a professional who can help you restore your mental resilience.

Don't let discomfort or shame slow you down from getting help. Most people wait way too long. What they don't understand is that most mental health issues are completely fixable.

And some are even preventable, if you learn to monitor your mental state, and have a steady routine for managing your mental wellness.

But no matter how diligent you are, you'll need a solid back-up plan in case life really throws you for a loop.

Now, you may find yourself in a situation where you use alcohol, drugs (or another addictive substance or behaviour) because it feels like a needed coping mechanism. But ultimately addiction can only tear you apart, so find the strength to tackle it head on. With the right help, you can find new ways to cope.

Key Point
Have a plan and a back-up plan for managing your mind.

Silence the Stigma

Let's switch a gear and talk about your team. As a leader, you are in a position to help silence the stigma associated with mental health. I ask you to take on this role. Educate yourself. Acknowledge the struggle. Talk about it with family, friends and your team.

Ultimately, mental health is no different than physical health. People just respond differently because of the stigma.

If someone breaks a leg at work, everyone knows exactly what to do: go to that person, comfort them, stabilize them if you can, and call the paramedics.

But if someone at work has a breakdown, an emotional outburst, or develops an addiction, everyone freezes. People retreat or say unhelpful things. No one knows who to call or what to do. So often they do nothing.

This is how tragedy happens.

The reality is we are all just one or two life events away from a mental health crisis. So be prepared to handle issues when they arise for you, and the people around you. There is a path back to mental wellness.

Simple Summary

It's as essential to take care of your mind, as it is your body.

〰〰〰〰 *STORY* 〰〰〰〰

Colin is a lawyer with a classic, high-performing personality.

He's programmed to win. He has the nature of a hunter, and it's served him well.

Like many execs, Colin sincerely tries to take care of himself. His work hours are intense, but he eats well, plays tennis regularly, and enjoys a lot of personal travel.

One Friday afternoon I got an unexpected and frantic series of texts from Colin, asking if I could talk right away. It wasn't his style to panic, so I knew something was wrong.

I explained via text that I was in a session, then on a plane home, and asked, "Can we chat Monday?"

He responded, "How about tomorrow – Saturday – at 7am?"

And so I knew something bad had happened. In the many years I had worked with Colin, we'd never spoken on a weekend, no matter what was going down.

It turns out Colin made a very public mistake on a big project for city government. Nothing like this had ever happened to him before, and it shook him to the core.

At times, I could barely make sense of what he was saying. He was overcome with anxiety. He had lost his ability to think rationally and see beyond the present crisis. He felt hopeless and ashamed. In his mind, his career was over.

But I wasn't concerned about his career. I was concerned about his mental state.

We carefully, slowly, talked through the situation.

I learned he'd been working longer hours for the past few months. His tennis schedule had fallen by the wayside, and he hadn't had a full night's sleep in more weeks than he could count. He let his eating habits slide – sometimes eating junk food, sometimes not eating at all. His usually sharp mind was murky and dull.

It took some time, but working with his doctor and with me, Colin got himself back on track. He has a new, more rigorous game plan in place for self-care and he's back at his peak.

Now, without fail, Colin plays tennis or works out at least 3 times a week. Plus, he goes on a bike ride or hike every weekend. He journals for 15 minutes every other day. And, very importantly, he gets a minimum of seven hours of sleep a night.

His successful career certainly isn't over—and with his new approach, I think, in many ways, it's just beginning.

Colin's story is far from unique. I've seen variations of his story at least a hundred times over throughout my career.

The pattern is entirely predictable. People get busy, stop taking care of themselves and as a result they're in a weakened mental state. Then life throws them a curveball.

It's neglecting the most basic things that messes people up – not eating well, sleeping well, or calming the mind.

The remedy is always the same: get professional help, and recommit to your Resilience Rituals.

Six Steps to Mastery

MENTAL HEALTH CONTINUUM MODEL

HEALTHY	REACTING	INJURED	ILL
Normal mood fluctuations	Irritable/impatient	Angry	Angry outbursts / Aggression
Calm & takes things in stride	Nervous	Anxious	Excessive anxiety / Panic attacks
Good sense of humor	Sad / Overwhelmed	Pervasively sad / Hopeless	Depressed / Suicidal thoughts
Performing well	Displaced sarcasm	Negative attitude	Over insubordination
In control mentally	Procrastination / Forgetfullness	Poor performance / Workaholic Poor concentration & decision-making	Can't perform duties, control behavior, or concentrate
Normal sleep patterns Few sleep difficulties	Trouble sleeping Intrusive thoughts / Nightmares	Restless disturbed sleep Recurrent images / Nightmares	Can't fall asleep or stay asleep Sleeping too much or too little
Physically well	Muscle tension / Headaches	Increased aches and pains	Physical illnesses
Good energy level	Low energy	Increased fatigue	Constant fatigue
Physically and socially active	Decreased activity and socializing	Avoidance / Withdrawal	Not going out or answering phone
No or limited alcohol use Gambling	Regular but controlled alcohol use Gambling	Increased alcohol use Gambling is hard to control	Alcohol or gambling addiction Other addictions

1. **Notice when stress starts to crack your armour**

   A certain amount of stress increases performance, but you need to know when you, or someone close to you, crosses that threshold. Everyone has a breaking point. I recommend a tool called the Mental Health Continuum, which is used by mental health associations around the world. It's an easy way to assess mental state and spot warning signs fast.

I'll give you a brief summary here, but I urge you to check out the full version at *lawrenceandco.com/books*. I extend my gratitude to Cameron Keller of Kaleidoscope Consulting, who introduced me to this incredible tool.

Mental Health Continuum

HEALTHY

Normal mood, sleep, social activity, energy level, performance, physical wellness.

REACTING

Nervousness, sadness, trouble sleeping, tired, low energy, tension, decreased social activity, procrastination, muscle tension, headaches.

INJURED

Anxiety, anger, pervasive sadness, hopelessness, restless sleep, fatigue, aches and pains, decreased performance, social avoidance or withdrawal.

ILL

Excessive anxiety, easily enraged, depressed mood, unable to fall or stay asleep, exhaustion, physical illness, unable to perform duties, absenteeism, isolation, avoiding social events.

A well-balanced person spends most of their time in the green zone. In my experience, most leaders visit the yellow and orange zones on a somewhat regular basis, and when things get rough, dip into red. I know this is true for me, and for many executives I coach.

I use this framework with my clients and it's incredibly common for someone to suddenly realize, *"Holy smokes, I'm orange right now."* It's an immediate reality check.

Here's the most important thing to know: no matter where you are on the spectrum, there is *always* a path back to the green zone.

When people are orange or red, mental wellness can feel like a distant reality, or even impossible. That's why these zones are dangerous. You don't have perspective. Your unsettled state seems permanent.

It's not. You *can* get better.

But you'll need a hand from a professional to see your way back to mental wellness.

Action

Review the Mental Health Continuum: What zone are you in right now?

_____

If you are in the green or yellow zone, make a list of things you can start doing (and/or keep doing), and stop doing (or do less) to strengthen your mental health. Refer to your *Resilience Rituals* from Chapter 3 – these are the activities to start doing or do more often.

START (OR DO MORE OFTEN)

1.	
2.	
3.	
4.	
5.	

STOP (OR DO LESS OFTEN)

1.	
2.	
3.	
4.	
5.	

If you are in the red or orange zone, make an appointment with your family doctor or a mental health expert, to get back on track. There's more information on this in point four of this chapter.

2. Be aware of major life events

There are certain life events that can throw even the most resilient person for a loop. Even one can be shattering. But if someone experiences two of these in close proximity, it's a definite reason to be on alert for warning signs on the Mental Health Continuum.

Major Life Events

Any of these events can trigger a mental health issue:

- Job loss
- Loss of a career dream
- Death of a parent or grandparent (even if elderly)
- Miscarriage
- Abuse
- Sickness or injury (even minor ones that affect lifestyle)
- Sickness or injury of a loved one
- Ending a relationship
- Key support person moving away
- Financial loss or crisis
- Major conflict
- Lawsuit
- Significant mistake
- Getting a new boss
- Loss of a pet
- Kids leaving home

Action

a. If you're facing one or more of these issues, check in with yourself...are you ok?

- If all is well, great. But keep an eye out for anything unusual.

- If all is not well, go to point four of this chapter and seek help.

b. Is anyone in your life facing one or more of these issues right now? How do they seem to be handling it?

- As above, if all is well—awesome. Watch out for anything unusual.
- If all isn't well, read point four and seek help.

3. Do some mental spring cleaning

Most people have at least one major trauma they need to clear out of their system by the time middle age hits; some have many.

You may know past traumas affect you in some way. They may rear their ugly heads when you are maxed out, or quietly float about in your thoughts. But it's also possible they affect you without you even knowing it, lurking beneath the surface of your consciousness.

It's important to review your life history, note your major traumas (use the Major Life Events List above for guidance), and ask yourself a tough question for each one: Is this an open or healed wound?

If your father died 20 years ago, and the pain of that loss remains sharp, it's an open wound, despite the passage of time. If it's hard to think or speak about a past event, it is an open wound that needs to be healed.

I recommend seeking expert help to make the healing process faster and easier, even though it may be possible to heal major wounds on your own.

Action

Review the Major Life Events list. What past events might be troubling you beneath the surface?

MAJOR LIFE EVENT	OPEN OR HEALED?
1.	
2.	
3.	
4.	
5.	

4. Know who to call

Make sure a good mental health professional is on your contact list, just a text away at any time.

Then whenever you find yourself in the orange or red zone on the Mental Health Continuum, you know precisely what to do. Call this specialist.

It's helpful to know your company's benefits program ahead of time because counselling services are probably covered.

If you find yourself lacking a trusted professional, see your doctor for a recommendation.

When someone else is in emotional distress, it's important to be realistic about the role you play. Unless you are a mental health pro, don't take on the task of being their primary source of advice and support. You wouldn't attempt to fix a fractured femur or clogged artery. Experts exist for a reason.

That's not to say you shouldn't take action—*do*. Let it be your role to make sure a professional gets involved and, of course, offer kindness.

Action

Which mental health pros can you call if an issue arises
for you or someone you know?

a. _____

b. _____

If you're not sure, find someone in your network to con-
nect you with an expert. If you are not sure who to ask,
your doctor is a safe bet.

5. Take preventative measures

Your Resilience Rituals are a powerful starting point
when it comes to prevention. These are the activities
that calm and rejuvenate you. They release the pressure
valve on stress.

In general, research says regular mental health mainte-
nance includes:

- **Exercise:** A regular exercise regime makes a big
  difference in mental health. It has to be something
  you enjoy—a team sport, jogging, a gym workout,
  hiking, yoga, swimming...whatever you are inspired
  to do consistently.
- **Eating well:** Your body reacts to the food you consume, and your mind responds to your body. So take
  this seriously. Eating junk leads to dark places. It
  destabilizes your blood sugar levels, making it hard
  to regulate your mood. You will feel better mentally
  with healthy food in your system.

- **Clearing your mind:** You need to regularly clear worries and spinning thoughts from your mind. I've found that journaling and meditation are the two most effective ways to do this. I journal regularly. In 15 minutes I can go from stir-crazy to calm and focused by pouring my thoughts onto paper. This is similar to a juice cleanse for the body. It rids your mind of toxins.

- **Having social connections:** The love and companionship of other people is fundamental to human existence. Make spending time with people close to you a priority. It will help you keep things in perspective.

- **Doing things you enjoy:** I know, I know – you love work. So do I. But mental wellness also requires experiencing things that give you the kind of amusement and wonder you experienced as a kid. These things will be specific to you. For me, it's boating and car-racing with family and friends.

- **Talking to someone:** Do this sooner rather than later when issues arise. Do not be alone with dark thoughts or anxiety. Reach out. This is why it can be so helpful to have a coach you trust. Your coach can be an unbiased sounding board for personal and business matters, and help you find the right solutions.

But it's crucial to understand that doing these activities does not make you immune to mental health issues when major life events occur. It's very likely you will need support in those situations.

Action
Which preventative measures do you need to start, or do more often?

PREVENTATIVE MEASURE	WHEN/HOW
1.	
2.	
3.	

6. Have coffee talks

When you're comfortable with your knowledge of the Mental Health Continuum, and you've got your own plan on track, you can be more aware of the state of those around you.

You may start to notice subtle things in people that may indicate their mental state –like changes in appearance, attitude, social activity, work attendance or substance use.

You may begin to get a sense of when someone you know well is headed for trouble. This is the time for a coffee talk. Make time to chat with the person outside the office, where they're more likely to open up about potentially difficult topics.

All you have to do is gently say that you've noticed something seems different about them, and you're wondering if there might be something really stressing them out. If they open up and share something, listen and be compassionate. People can benefit greatly from having someone hear and understand their situation. Sometimes that's enough.

If appropriate, you might tell them about the Mental Health Continuum, and your personal experience with slipping into the Yellow and Orange zones. See where the conversation takes you. Be a calm, listening presence. If it looks needed, point them toward a trusted professional, or offer to help them find one.

Action

Who might need a coffee talk with you this week?

_____

You Need to Work on Your Mental Health if Any of These Apply...

1. Your mind is out of control. It stops you from feeling good or making good decisions.
2. Past events stay with you and haunt you over and over again.
3. You're anxious or angry to the point it gets in the way of your life.
4. Addictive behaviour is a coping mechanism. The addiction increases over time.
5. You're stressed to the point of hurting your performance.

Gut Check

How skilled are you at managing your mental health?

On a scale of 0 (low) to 10 (high): _____

8

Learn Like Your Life
Depends on It

"The man who does not read has no advantage
over the man who cannot read."

MARK TWAIN

There comes a time in every leader's life when you believe you've got business all figured out. When that moment arrives for you— watch out.

You are about to fall off a cliff.

Sure you know a lot of stuff, and your business experience is invaluable. But be realistic – the current pace of change in the world is insane. You need to keep up if you want to stay relevant and successful.

Whether your company is worth one dollar or a billion, you need to remain curious and humble. You still have a lot to learn.

When leaders tell me they're way too busy to invest time in learning, I tell them being stupid is expensive and dangerous. Make the time.

Key Point
You need to double your capability every three to five years to deserve the designation of leadership.

Otherwise you'll find yourself implementing strategies that were brilliant five or ten years ago, but radically misguided today. This can kick-start your tragic slide into obsolescence, until one day you're explaining to your beloveds why the board booted you to the curb, and you're selling off personal assets.

It doesn't have to come to this. You're clearly a smart person. Invest the energy it takes to stay ahead of the game.

The top 10% of Fortune 500 CEOs read an average of 24 books a year, according to a study by Dr. Brad Smart, author of *Topgrading*.

The world's leading companies send their teams to management programs at Ivy League schools. Some even build in-house universities.

If the best companies on the planet place such an emphasis on learning, surely you should too.

Simple Summary

Knowledge alone is not the point. You need to put what you learn into practice, or you're no further ahead.

Carrie couldn't figure out why her reputable, long-standing manufacturing company was now struggling to turn a profit.

Quarter after quarter, she and her executive team racked their brains, trying to figure out what was wrong. Their products were solid. Their clients were impressive and loyal. But after decades in business, profit now eluded them, and Carrie couldn't keep the ship afloat much longer.

When she brought me in to help, I required the entire executive team to read *Islands of Profit in a Sea of Red Ink* by Jonathan Byrnes. They were thunderstruck by this completely different way of thinking about profitability.

They no longer had to cycle through their tired and fruitless list of old ideas. They saw the light about their true product costs. They retired several underperforming products, and found ways to lower production costs on others. They increased prices where they needed to.

In no time flat the underperforming company increased its gross margin by 50%.

They just needed to think about profitability in a modern way. They needed to get out of their own heads.

To do this, Carrie and her team – and *all leaders everywhere* – need to tap into brains outside their immediate purview.

They need to read.

Most CEOs and executives simply don't read enough.

In fact, most leaders all but stop reading after their formal education. I'm talking about wildly intelligent, well-educated people who just don't take the time to keep learning.

So one of the first things I generally do with my clients is institute a policy of reading one book a quarter, as an executive team.

Carrie made this policy part of her corporate culture – to keep her team, and her company, from being stuck again by narrow, or out-dated ways of thinking.

~~~~~~

Five Steps to Mastery

1. Take time to learn

Leadership requires foresight. You need the knowledge and skills not only for where your business is today, but for where it will be three years from now.

If you're not well ahead of your business and the market, you're not a leader. The tail is wagging the dog.

It's so easy to get stuck in survival mode, learning only whatever is needed to get by. But what you actually need to learn is how to get ahead. That's strategic learning. And if you don't invest time in it, you'll remain in business purgatory: survival mode.

So maybe you need do a deep-dive in a new product area so you can expand your revenue model two years from now. Or maybe you need to become an acquisition expert to support your long-term plan.

Plan to amass knowledge that helps you thrive in the future.

Action

1. How many days a year do you currently invest in strategic learning? This may include reading books, researching online, watching videos, consulting experts; and attending webinars, workshops and conferences.

   Current days per year: _____

2. How many days per year do you feel you would need, to be at your best?

   Needed days per year _____

3. What's the gap between 1 and 2? This is the number of days you need to carve out for additional learning.

   Additional days per year _____

2. Pick your areas

There are literally thousands of topics you can study to help your business perform better. So how do you choose?

The core of your learning should focus on areas that directly relate to your role, your market and your business plan.

I suggest you break your learning plan into two categories:

Strategic Initiatives: Consider the top three to five strategic initiatives you are planning, to achieve your biggest long-term business goals.

What topics do you need to master to support these initiatives? Make it your mission to become one of the world's most knowledgeable people, in at least two of these areas.

Action

Use the Strategic Learning Grid to plan your learning initiatives.

STRATEGIC LEARNING GRID

TOP STRATEGIC INITIATIVES FOR NEXT 3-5 YEARS	WHAT WILL YOU MASTER TO SUPPORT THIS?	HOW WOULD YOU LIKE TO LEARN?	WHEN?
1.			
2.			
3.			
4.			
5.			

Personal Fascinations: Your mind is at its sharpest, and most creative, when you allow it to explore its wildest fascinations. I enthusiastically encourage you to think beyond obvious areas of study.

If you love butterflies, learn about butterflies. If you're riveted by Egyptian mythology learn about that. If you're a geology buff, go for it.

You will be amazed. Expanding your mind in seemingly random areas of interest is more than just personally satisfying. It causes synapses to fire. It sparks creative ways of thinking. It is guaranteed to make you a better leader.

What three topics personally fascinate you? Fill in the first column of Personal Fascinations Grid.

PERSONAL FASCINATIONS GRID

PERSONAL FASCINATION	HOW WOULD YOU LIKE TO LEARN?	WHEN?
1.		
2.		
3.		

3. Know your learning style

Some people absorb information easily through the written word. Others prefer video. Maybe you love attending workshops. Maybe you learn best in a one-on-one setting.

For general learning, I prefer audio books and conferences.

I listen to 25 to 30 audio books a year, and regularly attend select conferences with multiple speakers.

For serious, in-depth learning, I prefer to hire experts for compressed one-to-one sessions. I can't stand most courses – they are too slow for me to stay interested.

The key here is to know what works for you, and waste very little time (if any) on other learning methods.

If books don't work for you, listen to an audio book or watch a video instead.

Action

Fill out the 'How I would like to learn' columns on the Strategic Learning and Personal Fascinations Grids.

4. Fit learning into your life.

I know, I know. You don't have time for a bunch of learning. Who does? Like I said before, just make the time.

I fit a lot of learning in when I travel to see clients. Whether I'm at an airport, on a plane or in a car, unless I'm on the phone, you can bet I'm listening to an audiobook.

Some people read every morning, or before bed every night. Some take getaways dedicated to learning.

If conferences or workshops are your thing, begin each year by booking these events, like you do your vacation time.

The point is to commit. Make it happen.

How can you fit more learning into life? Think of the times in your life when you can incorporate learning (e.g. on your daily run, audio books and podcasts in the car and in the air, an hour before bed each night, a weekend getaway twice a year).

Action

Fill in the 'when' columns on the Strategic Learning and Personal Fascinations Grids.

Tip

This will sound crazy, but I listen to audiobooks at 50% faster speed using a function in iTunes. I highly recommend this if audio is your thing. It's a major time-saver, and I find the content more engaging at a faster speed. For the same reason, a speed-reading course is a worthwhile consideration.

5. Get a good ROL (Return on Learning).

If you consume a ton of information, but don't use it to offer more value to the world, I'd argue it's not really learning. It's entertainment.

You get the highest ROL if you apply what you learn right away. Do something different than you would have done before.

As you consume new information, take notes on what you plan to do with it. If you finish a book or leave a workshop without a list of to-dos (with all due respect) what was the point? You might as well have gone to a movie.

If you are a voracious, insatiable consumer of knowledge but you never apply it, stop learning for six months. Instead, put your mental energy on implementing what's already in your brain. Pick some key insights and test them.

Over the years my clients have created some smart ways to increase their ROL. Here are some of my favourites:

- **Read as a team.** Choose a book every quarter for your team. Have a discussion as a team about what you learned, and how to apply the best information. This makes the learning process collaborative and practical.

- **Reread.** This sounds strange, but it's surprisingly effective. I know a CEO who gets his team to read 10 books every year – eight of which are repeats, two are new. Books are reread for five years, and then taken out of circulation. Repetitive? Yes, but consider how much insight is contained in a really good book. Rereading lets you embed the learning into your corporate culture.

- **Make conferences count.** Whenever someone attends a conference, have that person present the most significant findings and recommendations to the leadership team. Too often insight from conferences goes uncirculated, or gets totally forgotten.

- **Hire the expert**. Spending days on end at a conference isn't always the most efficient way to learn. Sometimes you can get the same information in a fraction of the time for a premium cost by hiring an expert to work with you directly. This may be the wiser investment. This works particularly well if you're the kind of person who is bored to tears at conferences.

Action

What three steps will you take to double your ROL (Return on Learning)?

1.
2.
3.

You Need to Work on This if...

1. The ideas and insights you have are often based on experiences from 10 or more years ago.
2. You have no formal learning scheduled in the next 12 months.
3. You haven't read a book since you finished your formal education, unless it was required.
4. You haven't learned about a completely new topic in the last 12 months.
5. Learning is a survival tactic. You acquire knowledge to handle current situations, not to strategically prepare for the future.

Gut Check

How do you rate as a lifelong learner?
On a scale of 0 (low) to 10 (high): _____

9

Get Tough Feedback

*"The biggest single problem in communication is
the illusion that it has taken place."*
GEORGE BERNARD SHAW

The more you succeed, the more people LOVE your ideas.

Funny that.

The reality is, you're not actually that much smarter now
that you're successful. Your ideas aren't always blessed by the
stars. You're human, and therefore prone to mistakes.

Like anyone, you need honest opinions to keep you on track.

Key Point
Get the truth about your performance
and how you need to improve.

The problem is, people's opinions of you will be clouded by your success. Even when they don't agree with you, they may go along with your ideas, assuming you know something they don't.

Or worse yet, people may endorse your ideas to stay in your good books—job security and ladder-climbing being top of mind.

So take heed. Don't take all that glowing agreement at face value. When you're not in the room, opinions might be markedly different. You need to create opportunities to hear what people really, truly think.

Then – *and this is critical* – be gracious and humble. Tough feedback will only help you be a smarter leader.

Most leaders have one or two people brave enough to tell them what's what, straight to their face. Identify these people. Seek their insights frequently.

For everyone else on your team, you need to create an environment that helps people to express their true opinions. 360° reviews are useful for this.

By the way, if you're thinking to yourself right now, '*All of this is charming but I don't need other people's opinions,*' I wish you well. You'll travel a rockier road with only your own insights to fuel you.

Simple Summary

You can't be your strongest without the brutal truth.

Marco was an extremely unpopular guy, and he had absolutely no idea.

Just a few months into his tenure as VP Sales, I visited his company to discuss the 360° feedback for each executive. When I previewed Marco's results, I knew it would be a kick in the gut.

To this point, he'd known nothing but success in his career. Everywhere he went he was a superstar, and Mr. Popularity.

But now he found himself in a family-style, extremely tight-knit corporate culture. While he hit his goals out of the park, he didn't fit in at all.

Marco casually and frequently declined invitations to dinners and events with the executive team, because he considered attendance optional.

He didn't understand that these get-togethers were an integral part of the corporate culture. They were not aimless social events, and certainly not discretionary. They were about creating personal bonds.

In Marco's 360° feedback, a number of people said they tried to build a rapport with him – but he kept declining social invitations. They felt he was *choosing* not to build friendships. They were enraged and offended by his brush-offs.

I facilitated the group through a difficult, and sometimes heated, discussion about Marco's place in the company. His colleagues expressed their frustration.

Marco was stunned, and suddenly he saw their vantage point. He could see this corporate culture was different than past jobs. He needed to make a choice to fit in or leave.

It turned out Marco genuinely wanted to fit in and he made the decision to participate in the social aspects of the culture. Now you can find Marco hanging out with the executive team like they are lifelong friends.

I truly believe that, without the 360° process – and Marco's humility and willingness to change – his tenure at the company would have been extremely short lived.

Five Steps to Mastery

1. Find the truth-tellers

Some people are natural truth-tellers. I think it's genetic. Truth-tellers are wired to give you the awkward truth. They deliver news you don't want to hear, and most people don't want to tell you. They tip you off if funny business is going on. They alert you to cancerous issues. In my case, I inherited truth-telling DNA from a long line of brutally honest people on my mother's side. It's not always pretty. Some people are uncomfortable with me because of it, but I gotta be me.

My truth-telling DNA serves me well as a coach. The way I see it, if I have an insight that can help someone be a better leader, staying silent is a crime. Thankfully I've finally learned to bite my tongue in my personal life. Identify the people on your team with truth-telling DNA. Keep them close. Nurture these relationships. Encourage their honesty.

And, most importantly, ensure that you don't make their life difficult when they give you the straight goods. Like a reporter or spy, you must respect your sources and protect them.

Most companies have one or two truth-tellers at the top, reporting to the CEO. Often there are three or four more within the ranks of the team.

Action

Make a list of your current truth-tellers. Note how you will enlist them to give you even more honesty. Next, create a list of potential truth-tellers and how you will enlist them.

CURRENT TRUTH-TELLERS

NAME	HOW TO GET MORE TRUTH
1.	
2.	
3.	

POTENTIAL TRUTH-TELLERS

NAME	HOW TO ENLIST
1.	
2.	
3.	

2. Handle honesty well

When some people receive brutal honesty, they send an invisible, angry signal that it is unwelcome.

Do not be this way.

If you are, the people around you can quickly, and wisely, decide to stay silent. Massive financial and human mistakes happen when people can't speak candidly. You rob yourself of knowing the silly or misguided things you are doing.

So while it is human nature to protect yourself, you need to drop your defenses.

Listen the best you can. Try to understand. *Then say thank you.* I know this sounds simple right now but it can be shockingly hard.

If you slip up and respond defensively in the moment, find the person later that day and express gratitude. Tell them you appreciate their insight even though it may not have seemed that way at the time. Ask them to keep the honesty coming.

It can help to let people know how you like to receive information that is hard to hear. Maybe you prefer a private chat, a phone call, or email to put yourself at ease.

KEVIN'S TAKE ON DEFENSIVENESS

Toning down your defensiveness may be a life-long journey.

Even though I've been training myself for years to receive brutal honesty with grace, it's still tough at times.

I fully admit that I'm an aggressive, competitive personality, and my gut reaction is to push back when someone tells me something I don't want to hear. This still happens occasionally, but not nearly as often as it used to.

I've learned that if I give myself a bit of time to cool off, I'm able to quickly apologize for my rashness, and express genuine gratitude for the feedback.

Truth-tellers are gold. It's worth the humble pie.

Action

On a scale of 0 to 10, how gracefully do you receive brutal honesty?

_____

If you are less than a 10 (which 99% of us are), what can you do to receive the truth more gracefully?

1.
2.
3.

3. Extract wisdom via project reviews

It is easier to give feedback on a project than a person, at least when that person is present.

So your team will probably be far more candid if you request feedback on a project you've led, rather than your performance directly.

If you listen carefully, you can get clear insight into where you're falling short as a leader, and what you're doing well.

Project reviews are simply a smart business practice. They force a team to learn from every project they complete. People get smarter all the time without even trying. Keep your process really simple and really structured. Get the group to discuss only three things:

   a. What went well

   b. What did not go well (where you got stuck or had challenges)

   c. What you learned: three things you'll do differently next time

If people come prepared the entire discussion should take somewhere between 15 to 60 minutes, depending on the complexity of the project.

Remember this process is about *progress*, not perfection. No matter how much you learn and improve, there will be brand new insights the next time around.

Action

Which three projects can you conduct a project review on right away? Who should attend, and when will the meeting be?

PROJECT	WHO	WHEN
1.		
2.		
3.		

4. If you're going to do 360°s, do them right

Ah 360°s. Some people love 'em. Some people hate 'em. I'm in both camps.

Normally they're a complete waste of time, in my view. But, done properly once a year, they are phenomenal fuel for growth.

The trouble with a typical 360° is that you don't get qualitative, actionable information. Instead you get a bunch of statistical ratings that leave you wondering how to improve.

Another problem is that they are often completely private, and this leads to a lack of accountability. Of course opinions usually need to be anonymous, if you want to extract tough feedback. But the recipient (in this case, you) should publicly thank everyone for participating, and commit to making specific changes.

So take your 360's out of the shadows. Use a succinct, direct questionnaire that asks mostly qualitative questions about what you're doing well and what you can improve. You can get great insights by asking only your direct and indirect reports, or you can include peers and higher ups as well.

When you get the report, work with your coach (or another expert) to decide what actions you can take based on the information. Complete the 360° Action Plan below.

Then, quickly follow up with your team, share what you learned, and what you will work on over the next few months. Ask for their support. Tell them to call you out when you're not living up to your intentions.

Here are the questions that are MANDATORY for an effective 360°.

1. List three things I can do to continue to grow and improve.

2. What should I start doing, or do more often? Why?

3. What should I stop doing, or do less often? Why?

4. What should I do better, or differently? Why?

The Team 360°

Team 360°s are *only* for well-oiled, cohesive executive teams that are really brave of heart. This is master's level. Here's how they work: Collect 360° feedback anonymously. Then, get the whole executive team in a room, and review each person's report *together*. Yes...together. Fun times. Each exec agrees to take specific actions to improve his or her performance (see the template below).

This is an incredibly effective way to make people hungry and humble.

360° Action Plan

1. Three areas where you said I'm doing well

1.
2.
3.

2. Three things you said I need to work on

1.
2.
3.

3. I'm taking immediately action on _____, because

_____

4. Here's how I'm going to do it _____

5. Here's how you can help me grow _____

Action

1. If your last 360° was less than a year ago, look back to ensure you have improved in the needed areas. If not, complete the 360° Action Plan, and start tomorrow.

2. If your last 360° was more than a year ago, schedule one now.

5. Get a Coach

One of the most compelling reasons to have a coach is to have someone who will always give you the straight-up truth.

A coach objectively follows your progress, and will call you out if you're not meeting your own standards.

I can't count the number of times a client told me that my tough feedback set them on track for greater success or averted disaster. It's not that my insight was brilliant or unique. It's that I was willing to say what everyone else saw, too, but didn't want to verbalize.

It can also be easier to hear brutal honesty from a coach, because that's the very nature of the relationship. Most people find it feels different than hearing it from your team, boss or spouse.

If you don't have a coach, why not? The highest performers in sports, business and life have at least one.

Action

1. If you don't have a coach, get one. If you need assistance, I can probably help you source a good one in your region. Drop me a note at *kevin@lawrenceandco.com*.

2. If you do have a coach, get twice the value from that relationship by picking three things from this book you would like to master.

1.	
2.	
3.	

You Need to Work on This if...

1. You wonder how effective you are as a leader.
2. You can't name four people who regularly give you uncomfortable, but valuable, feedback.
3. You haven't sought opinions on your performance through a formal mechanism (like a 360° review) in the past two years.
4. You wonder what your board (or the person you report to) really thinks of you.
5. You haven't received uncomfortable feedback from your board (or the person you report to) in the past six months.

Gut Check

How do you rate at getting other people's opinions of your performance?

On a scale of 0 (low) to 10 (high): _____

10

Make Yourself Useless

"The growth and development of people is the highest calling of leadership."
HARVEY S. FIRESTONE,
founder of Firestone Tire & Rubber Company

At a very practical level, it's your job to help the amazing people you've hired become great leaders.

Do not view them as underlings or boots on the ground. See them for their talent and potential. Let them live up to their ability to deliver amazing results with little (or no) involvement from you.

> **Key Point**
> Build a team that delivers better results than you, without you.

To do this, you need to invest time hiring, teaching, coaching, challenging and providing feedback. When you help people grow, they gain the confidence and skills to manage day-to-day business without you.

For you, this spells freedom. You'll be able to spend your time on your company's big picture strategy and long-term growth.

Sure all of this may seem obvious, but it's remarkable how often leaders get trapped handholding mediocre players. Sometimes it's because they hate hiring, so they'd rather live with the devils they know. Others let personal loyalty cloud better judgment.

No matter the reasoning, you'll be forever limited unless you do what it takes to surround yourself with A-players who are *truly exceptional* in their fields, and a culture fit with your company.

People think A-players are four-leaf clovers, but that's not my experience. You just need elbow grease, and a proven hiring methodology to find the best of the best. Then, it's your job to keep challenging them, and investing in their growth.

Believe you can have a full team of A-players. Then accept nothing less.

Simple Summary

To have any chance at greatness, leaders must have high-performing, low-maintenance teams.

Anne is the CEO of a food company, and a leader who knows how to get things done. She is not shy about delegating, even in areas where she has solid competencies.

Anne started her company with a clear understanding that she needed to focus on her absolute strengths: strategy and recruiting. So when she was still in start-up phase, she made the bold decision to only hire experienced, top-tier executives in other key areas like sales, marketing and HR.

Problem was, she couldn't afford them.

So she decided to work with what she had, and found superstar executives who were willing to work on a part-time contract, because they were taking some downtime or working as consultants.

Some might consider this a risky move, thinking it safer to secure full-time talent. But Anne's view was that she wanted people dramatically better than her to fill those roles.

The risk paid off. Soon her little company had a powerhouse executive team, well beyond its years. Those part-time execs stuck around, and when Anne's company hit the $50 million mark, she brought most of them on full-time. By the time she reached $100 million, all were full-time.

Today, when it comes to running the business, Anne often comments, "I know this sounds nuts, but there's not much I need to do" – and that means she can stay focused on strategy.

Moral of the story: get creative, work within your means, and do whatever it takes to hire the absolute best.

Four Steps to Mastery

1. Pick your date

Choose the exact date you plan to be completely useless to your business.

This is the day you will be free to step out of the day-to-day operations, or sell the company entirely. Envision yourself walking out the door.

It's crucial to pick a specific date so you can clearly see yourself moving on. Without it, you'll remain intertwined in the business. You won't push yourself to build a solid, self-sustaining team.

Whether you actually leave is not the point. The point is to build a company so strong it would function effortlessly without you.

Action

Set a date that is relatively soon – no more than five years from now. A longer-term date won't inspire you to take meaningful action.

My Useless Date

My team will be so strong that I will be useless by:

_____

2. Honestly evaluate the performance of each team member

Properly evaluating your team is one of the most compelling reasons to get outside counsel from a coach or advisor. Objectivity is crucial, and it's easier for someone external to the company.

The companies I work with typically double the strength of their executive teams within 18 to 24 months of our starting date. This is largely because the CEO gets a clear, unfiltered view of the team, and what improvements need to happen.

Your goal needs to be that *all* of your direct reports are A-players, as well as 90% of the rest of your company. This may seem extreme, but you are not reading this book to learn how to be average or mediocre.

Here's a simple performance rating system to help you get clear on where you are today:

		PERFORMANCE	
		LOW	HIGH
CULTURE FIT	HIGH	B	A
	LOW	C	TOXIC A

A-player: fits the culture, and always delivers exceptional results with little or no management. An absolute pleasure to work with, and you wish you could clone them.

Potential A-player: appears to be an A, but has been in the role less than six months. Looks promising but it's too early to be 100% sure.

Toxic A-player: excellent performance, but regularly causes friction and drama as they don't fit the culture.

B-player: a culture fit with spotty performance.

C-player: doesn't fit the culture or deliver results.

Action

Rate each of your direct reports as an **A**, **Potential A**, **Toxic A**, **B**, or **C**. List why for each one.

DIRECT REPORT	RATING	WHY	ACTION
1.			
2.			
3.			
4.			
5.			
6.			
7.			

What percentage of your direct reports are A-players?

_____

Tip

My website is filled with extensive tools and exercises for evaluating your team. Visit www.lawrenceandco.com.

3. Live by the motto, 'You have to be an A to stay'

This is neither impossible nor ruthless. It's just common sense.

A-players are your greatest assets. They produce more results than two or three B-players, so invest what it takes to find and keep them.

Don't fall into the habit of neglecting them because they are so self-sufficient. It's vital to have your pulse on how they are doing at all times because A-players have two dangerous tendencies: boredom and overwhelm.

They will be bored to tears if you don't let them handle

increasingly difficult challenges. That's why a favourite question for A-players is, "Are you challenged enough? Too much?"

Having said this, most A-players will not cry uncle when they've exceeded their limit. If you push them to the point of overwhelm, they may cut and run.

The key is to strike a delicate balance. Keep them challenged. Make sure it's sustainable.

Action

What action can you take for each of your A-players to make sure each one is challenged enough, but not too much? Fill in the A-Player Grid.

A-Player Grid

A-PLAYER	ACTION
1.	
2.	
3.	
4.	
5.	

4. Help your B-Players become A-Players

While the majority of your effort should be spent hiring and grooming A-players, your B-players deserve the chance to move up the roster. They are a cultural fit and that's a significant starting point.

Often B-players just need development, confidence boosting, or a tweak to their role so it's more in their sweet spot. You may convert them to an A through coaching, mentoring and/or training.

Start with assessments for each B-player so you can identify their sweet spots (I recommend *DISC* and *StrengthsFinder*). Assuming their sweet spots fit your needs, see if you can tailor their roles accordingly. Whatever you do, don't set them up for mediocrity by forcing them into a sour spot. No one will benefit.

The key to transforming your B's to A's is to help them see their gifts, and accept their weaknesses. Just because someone wants to be in a management role doesn't mean they should be. If their true gifts are as a technician or individual contributor, that's the only way they will ever be an A-player.

It's your job to identify how people can thrive, and guide them to be their personal best.

Action

For each of your B's, identify an action that could help them evolve to an A-player.

B-Player Grid

B-PLAYER	ACTION
1.	
2.	
3.	
4.	
5.	

5. Quit making excuses for your Toxic A's. And stop hoping they will quit

Toxic A's are the result of failed hiring practices. They slip through the cracks disguised as A-players, wowing everyone with their fancy talk and big results.

They have the power to make a normal workplace feel like a war zone. They make A-players lose faith in you, and seek their fortunes elsewhere.

Toxic A's are the cancer of your culture. They are not a problem to be treated lightly.

Sure, they bring in tons of revenue or big results. Yes, they can be counted on to perform remarkable feats any time of day, any day of the year. They are heroic, but terrible people. Ok, that's completely not true.

They are *not* terrible people. They're just a terrible fit with the culture of your company, and that's bad enough. Their ill fit tarnishes your company's reputation in ways you can't even know.

They need to hit the road.

When you realize you have a Toxic A in your midst, you need to create a plan for their (hopefully swift) exit.

Cover your bases. Give them fair warning, and one last chance if you feel you have not been clear enough about your cultural expectations. This may well be the case since Toxic A's can be tricky to communicate with.

Follow employment law and HR procedures to the letter, but set those Toxic A's free no matter how enchanted you are with their talents.

Action

Identify the action for each of your Toxic A's. This is the final warning or date you will terminate their employment.

Toxic A Grid

TOXIC A	ACTION
1.	
2.	
3.	
4.	
5.	

6. Manage out the C's

People often get messed up by putting too much energy into C-players, diligently trying to help them improve. That's what you call throwing good money after bad.

Do not be soft with your C's.

Even if they somehow manage to improve their performance, you'll never force them to be a cultural fit.

Give them a fair shot, of course. Make sure you've clearly communicated the culture of the company, and the expectations of their role. If they still can't measure up, set them free so they can find a place where they are naturally an A-player.

Action

For each of your C's, list the action you can take. Either schedule a time to reiterate the company's culture, their role and what it will take for them to be a fit—or, if you've done this already, put the wheels in motion to set them free. Pick a date for their exit.

C-Player Grid

C-PLAYER	ACTION
1.	
2.	
3.	
4.	
5.	

7. Fire compassionately

If you're firing someone, it's because of *your own error in judgment*. Remember this. It's not someone's fault they aren't a fit with your culture, or adept at the job you hired them to do. If you hired well, you would have known this. Somehow you picked the wrong person (or let someone else pick them). Own that responsibility and act accordingly.

Treat the person you're firing with respect and compassion, not only for the sake of that individual, but for your whole team. Your team will judge you and the company based on how you handle sticky situations. Moments like this are a test of your character.

Make sure you've got your company's core values at heart, and its reputation in mind, before you act.

Would you be ok if your words and actions were headlines in the local news? If so, you are firing people the right way.

Of course, if someone is fired for behaving criminally, unethically or otherwise dramatically inappropriately, it is necessary to act quickly and firmly. But there's still no reason you can't be civilized, in most cases.

KEVIN'S TIPS FOR COMPASSIONATE FIRING

There is no perfect or painless method for firing someone, but some ways are better than others.

1. **Treat people fairly**. Give warnings along the way to clearly communicate they are not measuring up, and what needs to change. Document everything, and review what others have documented. Make sure everything is above board.

2. **Help people move on with dignity.** Help them find a job where they have a better shot at being an A-player. Or at least point them in the right direction. In this way, you empower them to move up, not just move on.

3. **Let them lead the story.** You don't need to destroy someone's reputation simply because they aren't a fit for you. Let them craft the story of their departure. Give them the option of saying 'quit' or 'retired' versus 'fired' when possible.

4. **Treat long-time employees generously.** Yes, there are laws about minimum payouts, but pay more when it feels right. Consider rewarding longevity and past glory with more than is legally required.

5. **Move quickly for their sake and yours.** Waiting will only deplete your energy, and prevent forward motion. Odds are the individual in question knows something is amiss, and needs a catalyst for change. Just do it.

8. Be ruthless about hiring.

Most hiring is *way* too casual, amounting to chitchat and a wild leap of faith. You probably wouldn't get married after some pleasant banter over cappuccino. Don't hire people this way either.

Too many hiring decisions are made on great first impressions, but this has little correlation to actual skill and talent.

If your hiring process is deep, methodical and unsentimental, your chances of landing A-players skyrocket.

You know how deeply you know someone after you've taken a long trip together? Yeah, that's how well you should know your candidates.

Seem impossible? Not at all. That's the level of familiarity you get with a super-thorough, ruthless hiring methodology like you'll find in Brad Smart's book *Topgrading* – make sure you get the third edition.

Don't let your HR people resist you on this. They may

dismiss the idea of using a methodology at first because it's unfamiliar. But the proof is in the pudding.

My final word of advice: before you draft that offer letter, put your candidates to work.

If someone says they are an expert in conflict resolution, bridge design, blog writing or programming, let them prove it to you.

This simple and obvious step in hiring is often missed. Seeing people in action is a sure way to separate the talkers from the doers.

So yes, hiring A-players takes time and scrutiny. But it's far less painful than hiring mediocre people and cleaning up the mess later.

FOUR FUNDAMENTALS FOR RUTHLESS HIRING

1. Use a proven methodology like *Topgrading*, which is a rigorous system of interviewing. It provides a set of simple questions, and a detailed statistical job description, so it's easier to see who is – and isn't – an A-player.

2. Use a personality profiling system (like *DiSC*) to understand your candidates' natural strengths and working styles.

3. Conduct on-the-job assessments before you hire. Get your candidates to show you the work they can do.

4. Talk to past managers going as far back as you can—at least 15-20 years for experienced executives. You can quickly tell from the tone of the conversation if the person was an A, B or C at each organization.

~~~~~~

Action

What three changes can you make to your hiring process to double your odds of finding A-players, and weeding out Toxic A's and C's?

1.
2.
3.

You Need to Work on This if...

1. Your team isn't chock full of A-players.
2. You cling to one or more Toxic A's because you think their results are worth the havoc.
3. Anyone on your team is a C-player.
4. Your interview process consists of a series of 60 to 90 minute interviews with clever or interesting questions.
5. You hire people without test-driving their talents.

Gut Check

How good at you at making yourself useless by hiring and getting the most out of A-players?

On a scale of 0 (low) to 10 (high): _____

11

Quadruple Your IQ

*"Surround yourself only with people who are
going to lift you higher."*
OPRAH WINFREY

In the sport of business, you are an elite athlete.

Like Lionel Messi, Mario Andretti, Serena Williams and
LeBron James, you need a devoted team of people advising and
supporting you in a variety of ways.

No superstar operates alone.

Do not get caught in the unproductive cycle of trying to sort
out every single challenge on your own. In childhood you were
probably conditioned to believe that if you ask for help, you're
copping out, or even cheating.

But as a leader, you need to be the kid who's seeking help
from the smartest student in every class. You're *supposed* to draw
on the knowledge and brainpower of others. This boosts your
oxygen supply and makes everything in life easier.

Napoleon Hill tells the story of Henry Ford, who had a team of experts he called a 'Master Mind'. Each expert was available at a touch of a button on his intercom. Henry Ford understood it wasn't his job to have all the answers. It was his job to know all the people who had all the answers.

It's a complete waste of time and energy to solve every problem all on your own. Some brainy person somewhere has already done tons of thinking and experimenting to solve the exact issue you're facing.

Find that person. Get their insight. Add them to your team of experts.

And by the way, you _must_ have a team of experts at your fingertips, just like Henry Ford. These people are grey matter on demand. Genius by the hour.

Key Point
Have a team of 24 amazing experts
literally a text away.

Your team should include a lawyer, accountant, business coach, psychologist and personal trainer, to name a few.

I can't stress this enough: don't choose any convenient expert (like the lawyer who works next door, or the accountant you've used forever and a day).

Choose people that are genuinely phenomenal. Choose people you genuinely respect (and hopefully like).

Find the best people you can afford, and program their numbers into your phone so you can text them the instant the need arises.

Even if you don't use these experts all the time, you *must* have them on hand.

As business expert and author Jim Collins says, when it's time to deal with a problem, your first question should be 'who' not 'what'.

Simple Summary

Get yourself a whole bunch of genius on tap, even if you only access it now and again.

~~~~~~~~~~~~ *STORY* ~~~~~~~~~~~~

For the life of him, Amit could not get his team on the same page about the company's most fundamental strategic decision.

They needed to determine if they were going to position their product as a high-end premium brand, or stay as a commodity. Even though they facilitated their own strategy camps and brainstorming sessions, they ended up exhausted, frustrated and no further ahead. They talked in circles, and never came to any conclusion.

The situation was very stressful for Amit. *He* knew what he needed to do – what was right for his business – but couldn't get the team to buy in.

When Amit came to me for advice I helped him to locate a consultant who specifically helps companies figure out if they have the goods to be a premium brand.

The expert guided the team through a strategic process. Together, they decided that, given their market circumstances, a premium brand strategy would be the smartest road to travel.

It wasn't that the consultant had all the answers. But he had a proven process and experience working with teams like Amit's, and that made all the difference.

It's now five years later. The company successfully relaunched its brand and is charging higher prices. It is buffered from an increasingly competitive commodity market.

Amit now uses independent experts far more liberally and strategically. He realizes the smart people inside his company aren't always the best people for every single challenge – and that sometimes an expert you haven't even met yet is the fastest way to a good decision.

Five Steps to Mastery

1. Find the gaps on your extended team
There is a wide, wide world of genius out there so don't be limited by your current roster.

Leaders too often rely on a small set of advisors, and only seek new talent when a specific (usually urgent) need arises. They lean on the people they know because it seems like the path of ease. Unfortunately it's also the path of mediocrity.

Cast a wider net. Take a look right now at what kind of wisdom you could use on your team.

The combination of experts you need depends on your own talents, your industry, and the specific circumstances of your business.

Action

Start by listing your current advisors in column one on the Expert Scorecard. Notice the areas where you lack experts. These are items for your to-do list.

EXPERT SCORECARD

EXPERTISE	CURRENT EXPERT	FIT (0 TO 10)	14 X'er (0 TO 10)
WORK EXPERTS			
COACH			
ACCOUNTANT			
LAWYER			
HR CONSULTANT			
MENTOR			
BANKER			

EXPERTISE	CURRENT EXPERT	FIT (0 TO 10)	14 X'er (0 TO 10)
LIFE EXPERTS			
PSYCHOLOGIST/COUNSELLOR			
TRUSTED FRIEND			
TRAVEL AGENT			
INTERIOR DESIGNER			
PARTY PLANNER			
TECHNOLOGY/SOFTWARE EXPERT			
SELF-CARE EXPERTS			
COACH			
DOCTOR			
PERSONAL TRAINER			
PSYCHOLOGIST			
PHYSIOTHERAPIST			
OTHER EXPERTS			
GREAT LISTENERS			
CREATIVE PROBLEM SOLVERS			

2. Believe fit matters

Your advisors might be the equivalent of rocket scientists in their given fields, but if you can't relate to them, they're of no use to you.

Expertise is not enough. You need to like or respect your advisors. All of them. Make sure you pick people you won't hesitate to call when issues arise.

When a CEO calls to inquire about working with me, I explain that if we can't fight and laugh like siblings and still respect each other deeply, I won't be a good match. That's what fit looks like in my world. But of course not everyone is like me.

You need to know your criteria. What makes someone easy for you to be around? What makes you enjoy someone's company? Your personal and corporate core values will guide this. If an advisor doesn't match your values, move on quickly.

Action

Fill in the 'Fit' column of the Expert Scorecard, rating your experts on a scale of 0 (very awkward) to 10 (easy to work with, and brilliant things come from conversations).

3. Use 14 X'ers (aka Don't be anybody's guinea pig)

Cheap advice is incredibly expensive.

Some people love to help even when they have no idea what they're doing. Don't let anyone experiment with your business. Get the very best advice you can afford.

Make sure your advisors are legitimate experts – true geniuses in their chosen fields. Pay the premium that goes along with that.

I call these people 14X'ers. They've successfully dealt with the exact problem you're facing at least 14 times before, and lived to tell the tales (good and bad). This is what genius looks like.

So if you're having a dispute with a former employee, don't seek the advice of a general corporate lawyer for $150/hour. Find the specialist in employment law who handles these situations every single day. Even at $800/hour (as long as your business model can support it), the specialist is usually the wiser and less costly decision.

Now, when it comes to certain particularly innovative areas of expertise (like technology or marketing), a 14 X'er may not have done the *exact* thing 14 times. But they will have 14 experiences of innovation relevant to your situation.

Action

Fill out the 14 X'er column on the Expert Scorecard to rate the genius level of your current advisors on a scale of 0 (novice) to 10 (brilliant 14 X'er).

4. Strengthen your team: add and upgrade

By now, your Expert Scorecard reveals a story about your business.

You may see glaring holes in your genius roster. You may find that you have several advisors who aren't really a fit for you, or that can't fairly be defined as geniuses.

Carefully listen to the story it's telling. It is the making of your genius-on-tap action plan.

Unless you already have a 14 X'er you trust and adore in every area, you have work to do.

Action

In which areas of expertise do you most need to *add* a genius? Circle your top two or three on the Expert Scorecard.

Which experts do you most need to *upgrade* because they are a bad fit, or not a 14X'er, and that area of expertise is currently important to you? Circle two or three of these on your Expert Scorecard.

5. Consider an advisory board

Advisory boards are a potent way for CEOs to pool insight for big strategic decisions. They are useful to any leader, but especially private companies who don't have a corporate board.

Ideally an advisory board meets three or four times a year. Like all your other advisors, they need to be a strong fit with you. Make sure you include at least one CEO who has already been where you plan to be in 10 years.

This person will be like a local guide, helping you navigate the terrain.

It's typical that people start their advisory boards with an obvious cast of characters (their current lawyer, current accountant, etc.). But you need to quickly move to include people who are much further ahead than you in the business world.

Actions

1. Pick a date when you plan to have your first (or next) advisory board meeting:

_____

2. Decide who will attend the first (or next) meeting.

1
2
3
4
5

3. Pick three people you aspire to have on your advisory board in the future.

1
2
3

You Need to Work on This if...

1. The full weight of every decision rests solely on your shoulders.
2. You have doubts about major, upcoming strategic decisions.
3. When you review the lists of self, work and life advisors, it's clear you have important missing links.
4. When you get stuck on a decision, you often don't know whom to call. Or it doesn't even occur to you to reach out to someone.
5. You dislike, don't trust, or hesitate to call your current advisors.

Gut Check

How well do you use genius on tap?

On a scale of 0 (low) to 10 (high): _____

12

Stop Being Chief Problem Solver

"Give a man a fish, he eats for a day. Teach a man to fish, he eats for a lifetime."

CHINESE PROVERB

Leadership is not *Jeopardy.*

Yes, your ego loves to answer questions and solve problems, but you're doing yourself and your team a major disservice if this is how you spend your days.

I know, in the moment it's faster and easier to answer a question and move on. It's hard to watch someone struggle. But if you take the time to coach people through their problems, you'll have far more freedom in the long run, and a much shrewder team.

Your job is to clearly articulate your goals and expectations. Beyond this, let people think for themselves. When issues arise, guide them to answer their own questions and make their own decisions.

Then you'll have the breathing space, time and energy to do the things that matter: focus on strategy and live your life. You can't create greatness if you're constantly sucked into everyone else's thinking process.

Key Point
Require your team to make 90% of decisions on their own.

This boosts your team's confidence. Expands their abilities. It forces them to be stronger leaders.

And you know what? Most of the time, they know the answer to the question anyway. They know the decision they want to make. They only ask you out of insecurity. They worry about messing up or disappointing you. Or sometimes they're just lazy.

The key is to develop a pattern of communication right off the bat that requires people to think through their own problems, and present you with possible solutions.

Then I suggest you do a curious thing: respond to their questions with *other questions*. Not with the intention of being elusive, but to help them develop the strategic thinking to become strong, independent leaders and decision-makers.

You can also gain incredible insight into how your team members think. You'll get a clear picture of how capable they truly are. You'll know whom to trust with bigger, more complex decisions.

In time, if certain people keep making questionable decisions or bad recommendations, you'll know you have a competency problem on your hands. This is no longer an issue of empowerment. Either they are wrong for the role, or wrong for the business.

Simple Summary

Make people think for themselves, and they'll get better at it.

~~~~~~~~~ *STORY* ~~~~~~~~~

Anthony not so secretly viewed himself as a superhero. I think the Batman cufflinks gave him away.

He always swept in at the 11th hour to save struggling teams from despair and failure. He resurrected dying projects. He turned disgruntled customers into cheering fans. Anthony *loved* to save the day.

He also believed that if he wanted something done right, he had to do it himself. So with his incredible drive and ambition, he took on almost impossible projects, worked crazy hours, and came home exhausted and frustrated.

As an executive, Anthony needed to make the dramatic shift from superhero, to *leader* of superheroes. He needed to put his energy into developing his leadership capabilities, and building a team of people capable of doing the work.

That shift was remarkably hard on the ego.

It meant letting other people take the glory. It required Anthony to focus on his team – to help them grow, and to shine. It meant hiring people who were truly capable of being amazing, with the sincere intention that they could even outperform him.

It took a couple of years for Anthony's transformation to be complete, but it happened. He built a world-class team of A-players, who are superheroes in their ability to drive projects and deliver results. He let his people have their own moments in the sun, without taking any credit for himself – and he dedicated himself to mentorship and education.

Now that his team is so rock solid, Anthony is charged with two of his company's most important strategic projects. He learned that letting go of being an everyday superhero opened up a whole new world of possibility.

Four Steps to Mastery

1. Explain the method to your madness

If people don't know why you don't answer their questions and solve their problems anymore, they'll be extremely annoyed with you.

Tell them ahead of time. Explain that decision making and problem solving rests primarily on their shoulders. 90% is theirs to do, with 10% of your input and approval.

Acknowledge that it may be frustrating and more time consuming at first, but it will boost their capabilities as leaders.

Note: You're not off the hook entirely. This method backfires if you don't have your own perspective, and answer appropriate questions. You'll need to have an opinion, give advice, and make suggestions.

Action

Who currently makes the decisions on your team?
Decisions made by me:

_____%

Decisions made by my team (together or individually):

_____%

2. Believe in the brilliance of your people

Trust that they know the answers, and can make excellent decisions.

Leaders get a bad rap for being control freaks, but it's hard to let go when you believe things go sideways without you. Ultimately it all comes down to trusting the A-players you've so carefully hired, and giving them more responsibility.

Even if you don't have an A-team yet, try trusting people anyway. You'll be surprised how often people step up when required.

When you believe people can figure things out for themselves, they often will. At the very least, they'll start to strengthen their capacity for strategic thinking.

Action

a. Who can you challenge to do more thinking on their own?
b. What can you ask them to make recommendations and/ or decisions about?

WHO	WHAT
1.	
2.	
3.	

3. Help people to break through the 'I don't knows'

People often seek help because they are stuck in a mental loop, not because they're incapable of solving the problem.

In these situations they actually know what to do (or have some decent ideas), but their brain is stuck in an unproductive mode. They've essentially shut off their thinking process.

Your job is to help them get unstuck. I have a technique I call *breaking through the "I don't knows"*.

A conversation goes something like this:

Team member: *"I don't know what to do about this. What should I do?"*
You: *"Let's say you had to make a decision about it by yourself by end of day today. What would your decision be?"*
Team member: *"I don't know."*
You: *"If you stop analyzing it for a moment, what does your gut say?"*

Team member: *"I can't say. I'm really not sure."*

You: *"Go ahead – it's ok. If you had to make a call on it right now, what would it be?"*

Team member: *Finally responds with insightful answer.*

It's the craziest thing. When you give people a chance, often the right answer (or a decent attempt) just pops out. But because they are convinced they don't know, you'll probably have to ask three to six times to crack through the mental block.

You may still need to offer insight or a broader perspective. But even so, that person will be walk away more confident in his or her abilities.

Action

Which team members ask a lot of questions they probably already know the answers to?

1.
2.
3.

4. Require people to present solutions

One of my favourite management tools ever comes from former US Navy captain David Marquet. He turned the USS Santa Fe from the worst performing nuclear submarine in the entire fleet to the best.

He never allowed officers to drop problems in his lap. They had to think through the challenge, consider possible scenarios, come up with a solution, and present their recommendation.

When they were ready for his approval, they articulated their chosen course of action with the words, "I intend to..."

His job was to simply say, "Excellent, proceed." Or if he had concerns, 'Have you considered x, y or z?'

Lo and behold, his entire crew transformed into a team of potent, thoughtful leaders.

Imagine how simple your life would be if your entire team worked this way. To me, this is leadership heaven.

Now, you may prefer a bit more detail from your team. You might require people to present three possible solutions, and their recommended choice.

But whatever your version is, start doing it _today_.

Action

Which team members should start bringing you their solutions and recommendations?

1.	
2.	
3.	

You Need to Work on This if...

1. You are bombarded everyday with people asking your opinion.
2. People ask you the same types of questions over and over again.
3. You're involved in many small- to medium-sized decisions because your team won't make a move without you.
4. You have a long list of unresolved issues and open debates.
5. You regularly get stuck handling other people's problems.

Gut Check

How skilled are you are at helping people become independent leaders?

On a scale of 0 (low) to 10 (high): _____

13

Teach People to Meet Your Standards

"Have no fear of perfection. You'll never reach it."
SALVADOR DALI

You need to get what you want—your business depends on it.

You wouldn't be where you are today without a keen intuition about what makes customers happy. That gut sense is absolutely crucial to who you are as a leader. You've used this sense to set the standards that make your company successful.

Never back down from these standards. For anyone. Ever. Greatness requires exacting standards, and your customers love you for this—even though other people think you're a pain in the butt sometimes.

As a leader, you need to get comfortable saying exactly what's on your mind, even when it's what no one wants to hear.

You cannot win if you accept mediocrity. So you need to be a bold, clear voice articulating what excellence looks like. This can (and should) be done kindly and respectfully.

Get your expectations out on the table early with employees, consultants, suppliers and other collaborators. When something isn't quite right with someone's performance, tell them right away. Don't let it fester, and then explode later from frustration.

Key Point
Tell people what you really expect and hold them to it without apology.

There's a shocking lack of honest conversation in the business world. It's an epidemic. Leaders have too many pent up opinions. Teams hang in the balance wondering how they're doing.

People want real feedback. They want to do the best job they possibly can, but need to know where the bar is set.

And please, don't bother sweetening hard feedback with forced compliments, before and after. People see this coming a mile away, and most prefer the simple truth.

Simple Summary
Great people will find a way to meet your tough standards.

 STORY

Alan runs a huge organization with thousands of employees.

For years, he was a slave to his inbox, fielding an unending stream of emails from his team. The problem was, Alan detests email. But he felt he couldn't tell everyone to communicate another way. The ask felt too big.

When the stress of his inbox began to impact his health and well-being, Alan knew something had to change.

Now he has clear communication requirements. His number one rule is: 'no surprises'. Unlike some CEOs who prefer a buffer until a situation is truly urgent, Alan wants to know what's what *all the time*.

His team now sends small and frequent updates using WhatsApp. No more lengthy emails. No long-winded conversations.

These micro-updates mean that Alan is always in the loop. He's never caught off guard. He can see problems brewing early, and rectifies them before they grow.

Yes, he scans WhatsApp a lot, but finds it efficient to take little moments, throughout his day to quickly get caught up, without stress.

This style of communication wouldn't fly for everyone, but it works for Alan – and that's what matters.

Five Steps to Mastery

1. State your expectations up front

Don't let people flail about guessing what makes you happy. It is a waste of everyone's time.

Get clear about the standards that matter to you most, and write them down so they can be easily shared with your team.

You know who's great at articulating their needs? Musicians. These people know how to get what they want. Van Halen is famous for an extensive written list of needs, including M&Ms at every venue – but 'absolutely no brown ones'. Mary J. Blige requires Red Vine liquorice, Diet Dr. Pepper, and Aveda candles wherever she plays. Think of your standards list as your very own tour rider. The more specific you are, the more likely you'll get what you want.

Your list should be required reading for everyone who works with you, including full-time employees, contractors, consultants and suppliers.

Make sure you include big picture stuff like your company's core values, with a simple explanation of what these mean. Your core values should give people a clear understanding of the behaviours that are acceptable to you. Don't bother with ambiguous, fluffy or stereotypical core values (e.g. 'superior customer service' and 'innovation'). Vagueness won't help anyone align to your expectations. Also make sure you include nitty-gritty instructions about your personal preferences. For example, I make sure my team knows I prefer text to email communication, and phone calls to in-person meetings.

Some CEOs stipulate that meetings should never exceed 60 minutes, and must end with at least five clear action items. Others have extremely specific guidelines about product development and delivery.

The key is to know yourself, and know what drives you crazy, when it's not done correctly.

Action

How do you really want people to work with you? List five things you wish everyone on your team would *always do*—or *never do*—when working with you.

1.
2.
3.
4.
5.

2. Practice requesting the little things that matter to you

This can help you become more comfortable with stating your standards in general.

If you're in a cab and the temperature is uncomfortable, request an adjustment. If you'd like a different side dish with your meal, go ahead and ask.

Yes, these things may seem insignificant. But you will be more satisfied if your preferences are met, and you will learn the powerful art of the polite request.

The operative word here is *request*. Demanding is decidedly less effective, and you'll just look like a diva wherever you go.

But if you request, people often go out of their way to help you. And if they can't, they have the legitimate option of saying no.

Getting what you want can (and should) be a civilized process. Notice your word choice. Notice your tone. Notice if you're open to another person's viewpoint.

With the right approach you can usually request, and receive, exactly what you need.

Action

What things do you tolerate on a regular basis that can be solved with a simple request?

TOLERATION	REQUEST
1.	
2.	
3.	
4.	
5.	

3. Practice graceful disappointment, and never lower your standards

People will try to meet your needs, and sometimes they will fail. You need to accept this reality and develop workarounds.

Backing down and accepting sub-standard performance is not the right approach. Instead, practice graceful disappointment and re-requesting.

I'll admit I'm an extreme case. I'm disappointed in the customer service I receive 98% of the time. If I didn't carefully monitor my attitude and behaviour, I would go through life as a big jerk. But this is no way to live, and it wouldn't help my cause.

When shoddy service happens in restaurants or stores, I do my best to be compassionate, and not take out my frustration on the person trying to help me. I remind myself employee training might be lacking. I remember that everyone has bad days. People are often doing the best they can.

I've learned to *calmly* explain when something isn't quite right, and make a specific request about how to fix it. I make sure my word choices focus on the outcome, not anything personal about the individual, or their performance.

Action

What kinds of situations cause you to lose your cool? Make a point to employ the method of a calm re-request the next time a situation arises.

SITUATION	RE-REQUEST
1.	
2.	
3.	
4.	
5.	

4. Up the bar and get more specific

As you go through life, you learn more about what works for you and makes you happy. It's ok to get pickier as you go.

When I first started public speaking many years ago, I had a brief but essential list of needs that I would send ahead to venues: a Lavalier mic, a projector and water. Now my list is longer, and far more specific, because I'm well acquainted with the vast assortment of things that are helpful to me—and that can go wrong. I'm not a diva about it – no one's sorting out brown M&M's. But I am clear about what I need to do my job well.

So I make sure venues have a back-up battery for the Lavalier, and a table for my laptop that's close to a power outlet. I ask that all A/V equipment has been tested before I arrive, and that a technician is there to meet me an hour before I speak. I request a pitcher of water without ice, and two glasses. The list goes on... very specifically.

The point is, now I know more about what I need to be successful. And people are usually delighted to accommodate me.

Action

What checklists do you need to create so people can help you be more successful in high-stakes situations?

MY HIGH-STAKES SITUATIONS LIST

SITUATION	NEEDS
1.	
2.	
3.	

5. Know when to fold 'em

Over time it will become clear who is capable of meeting your expectations, and who isn't. Even with patient requests and re- requests, you'll find some people can't meet the bar. It's just not in them.

In situations where you've been crystal clear, and someone can't deliver, you need to modify their role so they can deliver, or find someone else entirely.

Do not beat yourself up about this. Some people aren't a fit for you.

It's a big world out there. Someone else will be able to meet your needs. Break ties. Move on. Test out some other options. It will be possible to find someone who really gets you.

Action

Which team members do you need to...

Give one last chance to meet your expectations?

1.
2.
3.

Break ties with, and find an alternative?

1.
2.
3.

You Need to Work on This if...

1. You hesitate to say what you really want because you don't want to seem demanding.
2. You often accept results that are less than you expect.
3. You fix things so they meet your standards.
4. The same frustrations keep happening with the same people.
5. You regularly make do with less-than-ideal situations.

Gut Check

How skilled are you at graciously getting people to meet your high standards?

On a scale of 0 (low) to 10 (high): _____

14

Tackle Tough Conversations

"I prefer an ugly truth to a pretty lie."
SHAKIRA

Most leaders aren't nearly as tough on their teams as people think.

In fact, if you're like most, you've gone to great measures at times, to avoid conflict with your direct reports...because you care about these people. You don't want to offend anyone.

It's understandable. You're human. Most of us would rather have a root canal than say something difficult to someone we care about.

But the reality is, sometimes people do things that aren't ok. They do things that make you frustrated, uncomfortable or angry. You can't let important transgressions go unaddressed, or resentment will build up inside you until, one day, you snap.

Part of being a leader is to help people see where they've gone awry. The best way to do this is to let your emotions settle, and then address the issue head-on, within 48 hours of the incident.

Tough conversations like this are the nastiest annoyances you'll ever have to handle as a leader (see Chapter 5 on Toads). There's no way out. Just do what needs to be done and move on.

Key Point
Get tough conversations done within 48 hours.

The secret is to find language that makes it easier for you to deliver the information, and easier for the recipient to hear it.

Be direct *and* compassionate, not just one or the other. Focus on facts and feelings, not opinions. Opinions only lead to disaster.

Simple Summary
Get comfortable delivering the uncomfortable truth *quickly*.

STORY

Victor had a bit of a vengeful streak.

As CEO of a fast-growing tech company, he proved to be a capable leader in many vital ways. But, by nature, he found giving feedback very difficult. He was uncomfortable addressing performance or behaviour issues.

Victor channelled his frustration into The List: an ever-changing, ever-growing roster of employees with whom he had a bone to pick.

Employees and executives knew The List existed, but no one ever knew who was on it – or why. Every so often, without warning, Victor would eradicate someone on The List. Like a sniper in the night, he simply ended their career at the company.

People lived in fear.

Clearly the situation wasn't sustainable. And when Victor realized he was creating a culture of fear and distress, I coached him on how to give feedback directly to his team as soon as issues arise.

It took some time to overcome his discomfort, but using the Tough Conversation Model, he developed a new habit to address problems the same day they happen.

The List is ancient history. Facing his own fears made Victor a better communicator and leader. The corporate culture has shifted – people now focus on the work at hand, rather than fearing for their jobs.

Five Steps to Mastery

1. Wait a few hours until the emotion settles

When a member of your team says or does something way out of bounds, you may have a fiery instinct to respond rashly.

Most people know when they're about to say something they will soon regret. Even though a little part of you wants to say it anyway, wait. Let your mind calm down. Find a way to process your emotions within 48 hours without stifling them.

Sometimes a good night's sleep makes all the difference. Don't wait longer than 48 hours, unless you are still too frustrated to have a calm, professional conversation about it. As time passes, the issue will seem less important, but it isn't. Take action while it is front and centre.

Action

Who do you need to have a tough conversation with in the next 48 hours?

---

2. Schedule the conversation

Pop by the person's office and say something like, "Hey, I'd like to have a chat this afternoon. Would 3 pm work?" You can make the request by email (or text if you prefer), but make it clear you are asking for an in-person conversation.

Tough conversations—whenever possible—should

happen in person. They should *never* happen by email or text. Ever. These forums only amplify tension.

If distance is a factor, or there are other complicating circumstances, phone is acceptable, though not ideal. A video conference is better.

Initiating the conversation is a magical thing because then there's really no turning back. The ball is rolling. You're committed. It's happening.

At the appointed time, before you dive headlong into the conversation, start by re-confirming it's a good time to talk. If a crisis has suddenly emerged for the other person, don't throw a tough conversation at them. Check that all systems are go. Then proceed.

Action

What step will you take today to initiate a tough conversation?

---

3. Plan what you're going to say using my Tough Conversation Model

The Tough Conversation Model is the safest, fastest way to handle any tricky conversation. It is designed to keep your anger, frustration and discomfort in check. Without it, you might say heated things you later regret. You might create an unnecessary altercation.

Although you may be tempted to let your emotions fly, it's never worth the damage to a relationship. Your remorse will far outlast any fleeting satisfaction.

To create true understanding, your words need to be neutral and strategic. Planning gives you the space and time to choose words the other person is able to hear.

The Tough Conversation Model

1. **ASK PERMISSION**

   Make sure the other person is aware they are going to hear some tough information. Begin the conversation by stating this, so you're not blindsiding them. Make sure they are ready to hear you.

   Be brief and to the point. It should sound something like:

   "John, I'd like to talk to you about something that's a bit uncomfortable. Are you ok with that? May I have your permission to be really direct?"

2. **STATE THE INDISPUTABLE FACTS IN 20 SECONDS**

   With any problem, there are usually two or three facts, and approximately 427 judgments. Your job is to convey the facts. Keep all judgments to yourself.

   Judgments assign blame and, because of this, immediately make a conversation toxic. People get defensive when you drag your judgments into a discussion. This gets you nowhere.

   Don't weave a story around the facts, or assume you know the other person's motivation. These are your personal interpretations of what happened. Pure conjecture. Pure judgment.

   Because there are so few actual facts in any situation, it will take about 20 seconds to get them out on the table.

If it takes longer than that, you can be sure you've ventured into judgment territory.

Here's an example of how judgment sounds compared to fact:

Judgment (DON'T do this)

"You completely disrespected me in the board meeting. You're always trying to take centre stage. I know you want more funding for your department, but you had no business announcing our new product idea."

Just The Facts (Do This)

"I was taken aback when you announced our new product idea. I thought we agreed more due diligence is needed before we know if it's viable enough to present to the board."

3. **STATE YOUR FEELINGS ABOUT THE SITUATION**

From a calm, clear-headed place, state how the situation made you feel.

The goal isn't to create a touchy-feely conversation. Stating your feelings helps the other person understand why the situation needs to be resolved. It conveys the importance of the matter, and helps them get why you're frustrated.

Brevity is key. Your tone needs to be neutral, even though you're discussing emotion. Watch that you don't assign blame. Simply state your emotional reaction.

For example:

"I felt very uncomfortable. It was like we were suddenly rivals instead of on the same team."

4. **SUGGEST THE RESOLUTION OR MAKE A REQUEST**

You need to be abundantly clear about what will resolve the situation.

For example:

"I wanted to share this with you so that you understand my perspective. My request is that when we agree not to speak about something in a board meeting, we stick to it. If you disagree with me, let's talk it through beforehand so that we can go into the meeting united. What are your thoughts?"

Tough Conversation Plan

Create the plan for the tough conversation you need to have:

1. Permission: _____

2. Facts: _____
   _____

3. Feelings: _____
   _____
   _____

4. Suggested Resolution: _____
   _____

4. No matter what stick to your plan

Stick to the plan. Stick to the plan.

Stick. To. The. Plan.

You will likely find your conversation takes less than a minute (or some similarly brief period of time). People can't dispute the facts, and they can't dispute your feelings.

You have laid the groundwork for a civilized discussion, and a quick resolution to a tricky problem.

5. Have an open mind. Assume you are missing some key information

Even when your brain doesn't have all the facts, it likes to assume it does. Most brains have a tendency to believe their perspective is whole, especially when you are rattled.

The reality is you may not have all the facts. Approach every tough conversation from this vantage point, and *listen* to what the other person has to say. Assume you may be missing crucial information, rather than believing the other person is certainly wrong or spiteful.

When someone frustrates you, it's easy to see them as a villain. If you do, every word out of your mouth sounds confrontational.

This is not the route to a calm, clear resolution. It's not the route to understanding.

The way you feel walking into the conversation, and the thoughts that are in your head, set the energy in the room. If you truly want resolution, don't walk in feeling wounded and irritated. Be open to hearing a completely different, and equally valid, side to the story. Make sure to speak in a neutral, non-judgmental tone.

If you show up to peace talks with a gun in your hand, don't complain later when all hell breaks loose.

The Coaching Triad

Several years ago my coach and I accidentally invented a ridiculously useful method to get to the truth at hyper-speed. It's called the *Coaching Triad*.

It originated because I noticed some CEOs struggled to give tough feedback to their executives in one-on-one conversations. I also noticed huge disconnects between how people perceived the same situation.

To solve this, I started holding triad meetings with three people present: someone getting feedback, someone giving feedback and me, an unbiased third-party.

Here's how to hold a *Coaching Triad* meeting

a. Schedule a 20 to 30-minute meeting with the team member you want to give feedback to, *and* an unbiased third-party coach from outside the company.

b. In the meeting your team member speaks first. They get five to seven minutes max to share two things: how they are growing as a leader and what they believe they need to improve to be more effective.

c. Next, you get five to seven minutes max to say what the person is doing well, and what they need to focus on and accomplish to improve their performance.

d. Then the coach summarizes what's been said, and clarifies if needed. The coach facilitates agreement on the areas where your team member will take immediate action for improvement.

e. After the meeting, the team member and the coach work together on a plan to help them grow.

The communications model cuts straight to the heart of the matter. There's no time for long-winded explanations, or beating around the bush. Because of this, there is great clarity. People know where they stand.

There's something about the combination of directness, simplicity, limited time and formality that produces great candidness.

To work this model needs to be followed strictly. It *can't* be done in a one-on-one conversation. You *can't* toss in other topics. Be rigorous and you get profound results.

You can find the Coaching Triad methodology here: *lawrenceandco.com/books*

You Need to Work on This if...

1. You say nothing when things go sideways.
2. You explode when people anger or disappoint you.
3. You let little frustrations build up until you reach a breaking point, and rashly fire someone.
4. People get defensive or emotional when you give feedback.

Gut Check

How skilled are you are at quickly giving tough feedback?
On a scale of 0 (low) to 10 (high): _____

15

Love the Lessons

"I never lose. I either win or learn."

NELSON MANDELA

Leadership is supposed to be painful sometimes. This is normal.

You're not alone if you have sleepless nights, if you question your sanity, if sometimes you feel like you are breaking.

This is part of the reason major achievements are so satisfying. You know deep in your heart how much you've earned those wins.

Pushing through your pain is what causes you to evolve. It motivates you to get smarter. Your struggles test you, forcing you to prove your true commitment to your goals.

Key Point
Appreciate that painful experiences make you stronger and smarter.

But without the right perspective, the struggles of leadership can lead to a dismal place. You can get stuck in the pain, locked in a mental loop about how you've been done wrong, and the world is against you.

You need to learn how to make a fast mental shift to a healthier perspective, so you don't get stuck in the darkness.

I call this switching from a 'woe is me' to a 'wow!!' perspective. You know you've made the shift when you are genuinely excited about what you're meant to learn from a difficult experience, knowing it will make you stronger.

The secret to this switch is to find the meaning behind your pain.

Meaning changes everything.

It gives you perspective. It allows you to love the challenges of leadership. It creates the mental space for you to change. It provides the path for you to become wiser and sharper, instead of worn down and resentful.

If you're in a state of 'woe is me', you can't move forward. Woe leads to inaction and a lack of creativity. You waste energy seeking sympathy, rather than forging ahead with optimism and passion.

Let's be real: leadership isn't for the meek. It's for people like you who are bored with a normal existence. It's for people with a burning desire to improve.

If you can see every difficulty for what it actually is – an opportunity to evolve – your entire experience of life changes.

Simple Summary

Develop the skill to stare challenges dead in the eye, and say, 'wow!' instead of 'woe!'

Alessandro created a debacle that would have ended the career of a lesser CEO.

He refused to fire to a long-time CFO who, in my opinion, needed to be let go. Whenever I suggested finding someone new, Alessandro persisted. With so many other pressing concerns to deal with, surely the CFO was good enough for now.

Then, one fateful day my phone rang, and it was Alessandro. Something had gone seriously wrong with his company's cash flow, and he needed to raise $2 million in 10 days, or he would be out of business.

The bank wouldn't cover him, so this proud man went, hat in hand, to ask family and friends to lend him money. Knowing him to be an honourable guy, people came through. He raised the $2 million, and lived to tell the tale.

When we sat down to discuss it afterward, he described it as the most humiliating experience of his life.

I asked him the question I always ask when something goes painfully wrong, "What is totally perfect about this situation?" It's my way of pushing people to see what lesson they are meant to learn.

Alessandro quickly realized that this near-disaster was the catalyst he needed to get the right team in place, to get a deeper understanding of his financials, and to stay on top of them.

He acted quickly and hired a rock-star CFO who helped him restructure his business model. It only took 6 months for Alessandro to pay back his friends and family.

The real kicker to the story is that the profit of the company now sets records, year after year. It was a tough lesson to learn, but Alessandro now understands he needs to focus on people, profit and cash position with the same attentiveness as big picture strategy.

Three Steps to Mastery

1. Notice the upside of pain

It's easy to dwell on the downside of struggle – to let anger or frustration blind you to the other angle on your story. Your struggles have made you sharper, wiser – very likely a better person and better leader.

In this way, struggles are magnificent, and need to be honoured. Pain offers knowledge, but it can only evolve you if you let it.

The mind tends to believe it's always known what it knows right now. It takes for granted the significant knowledge gained from your struggles. You need to find a way to see this contribution.

Action

By this point in life, you've had many struggles that shape the person you are today. List five of the most painful challenges you've had to overcome so far in life, and how you grew stronger.

PAINFUL CHALLENGE	HOW YOU GREW STRONGER

2. Get your money's worth

Life is the best teacher you'll ever have. It's constantly sending lessons your way. The question is: are you getting them?

When things go 'wrong', you can default to resistance, or you can say, 'Excellent, here's the next course in my life curriculum.'

That's how you switch your brain from a story of woe to a story of wow.

You can turn everything around with this simple mental shift. With every obstacle ask, "What am I meant to be learning?"

Train your brain to look for the lesson, and be grateful for it, because it's a chance to be better. That's how you start feeling ok again, and ready to move forward.

This applies to life's biggest and smallest challenges.

Action

What current challenges are you deeply frustrated about? Fill out the Current Challenge Grid with the intention of understanding the process of moving from 'woe' to 'wow'.

CURRENT CHALLENGE GRID

CHALLENGE	WOE STORY	WOW STORY
1.		
2.		
3.		

3. Change your story from 'woe' to 'wow' when it matters most

The story you tell yourself about any situation is about 1% fact, and 99% interpretation. You completely control the interpretation.

Unfortunately, most people have not mastered the skill of consciously choosing the interpretation of a situation. Instead they react, and go wherever their emotions lead them. Learning to take charge of how you interpret your life events is one of the biggest opportunities you have to improve as a leader.

So if a trusted business partner runs off with your biggest clients and best ideas, how do you tell that story?

- You could tell this as a story of betrayal, and agony to rebuild your business from scratch. That's what a story of **woe** sounds like.

- You could tell this as a story of how you rethought your whole business model, allowing you to leapfrog the competition – and how you learned to choose partners of integrity, not just talent and connections. This is a story of **wow**.

Funny thing: neither story is truer than the other. Each is about 1% fact and 99% interpretation. It's entirely up to you which one you choose.

A story of wow helps you grow, and have a positive feeling flowing through your veins. It helps you to move forward. It inspires action and learning.

But you should know, woe stories are far easier to cling to. Everybody loves a good woe story. People will want to hear your woe stories so they can sympathize and commiserate with you. It's easy to be lured in by this attention.

It takes massive courage and diligent practice to switch to a wow mentality. This is an absolutely fundamental skill to master if you want to win at leadership and in life. Elite-level leaders quickly find the wow in any situation. When a curve ball comes hurtling their way, their response is, "Wow, this is going to be intriguing and a great chance to learn. Let's do it!"

Of course, even the strongest minds occasionally freak out at a particularly enormous, or seemingly ill-timed challenge. Sometimes you need more time than usual to wrap your head around a situation. That's ok. The key is to avoid a pity party, and make your way to wow as quickly as you can.

As you practice the art of wow, it gets faster and easier.

Action

Look at the challenges in the previous section, and list what your current woe story is. Then, what the wow perspective could be.

The Venting Template

For most people, the natural process of releasing the pain of challenging life events can take years. For some, the pain turns into permanent toxicity.

The Venting Template is designed help you switch from a 'woe' to 'wow!' mentality. It helps you quickly release the pain and anxiety of a mild to moderate issue, to uncover the good that came from the situation, and to make this your dominant memory. For big or intense situations, you can still benefit from professional help.

The Venting Template is my go-to method for mental cleansing. It efficiently takes you through the full emotional cycle.

For the life of me I can't recall the person who shared this tool with me, but I send credit and thanks to that wise soul.

How to Use the Template

Let it rip. Let everything out. Write about a page of content for each of the seven sections.

Write stuff that you don't even want to write. Write it in code if you need to. Then, get rid of it in whatever way feels right to you, to kick those toxins right out of your system.

You might need to go through this exercise a few times to fully process the pain. In the end, you have flushed out all the crap, and only the gift remains.

Situation _____

1. I hate it when...
   - I can't stand...
   - I'm angry that...
2. It hurt me when...
   - I feel sad when...
   - I feel disappointed about...
3. I was afraid that...
   - I feel scared when...
   - I'm afraid that...
4. I'm sorry that...
   - I did not mean to...
   - Please forgive me for...
5. All I ever wanted was...
   - I want you to...
   - What I want for you is...

6. I understand that...

  • I appreciate...

  • I love you because...

7. I forgive you for...

  • I thank you for...

  • I'm better off now because...

Action

What situation do you most want to change from a 'woe' story to 'wow' story? Use The Venting Template to make that shift.

You Need to Work on This if...

1.   You are generally unaware (or in disbelief) that 99% of your story, about any challenge, is pure fabrication.

2.   You quite easily get stuck in 'woe' thinking about past struggles, even though they probably made you stronger.

3.   When a new struggle arises, your mind quickly starts to produce thoughts of woe, about how challenging your life is, and how you wish things like this would not happen to you.

4.   You don't get your lessons. You keep facing the same types of struggles, again and again.

5.   When obstacles arise, you get stuck, and don't move forward for a long time.

Gut Check

How good are you at finding the 'wow' in your challenges at work and in life?

On a scale of 0 (low) to 10 (high): _____

16

Keep Going For It

"We don't stop playing because we grow old;
we grow old because we stop playing."
GEORGE BERNARD Shaw

The very best leaders know deep down they can handle absolutely anything.

This kind of confidence comes from staring monsters dead in the eye. It comes from walking toward fear.

To achieve this confidence, you need to consciously choose to do things you think you can't. Keep scaring the crap out of yourself. You'll be a stronger, sharper, more confident person – and you'll have a far more intriguing life.

The reality is humans are extraordinary, and have an unending ability to evolve. But if you don't push yourself hard enough, your true potential will remain untapped.

Key Point
Keep creating opportunities to be a
novice learning from masters.

It's a strange irony that success makes you weaker if you're not careful.

When we're young, life is always about trying new things. It's all about experimentation.

But as a leader, you probably spend most of your time in situations in which you are already masterful. You may not let curiosity guide you to unknown terrain as you did earlier in life.

This leads to a skewed and dangerous perspective that you've got life nailed; that nothing can bring you to your knees. While this may be cozy, it definitely won't put you at your cutting edge.

Every leader should be humble and hungry, no matter how accomplished. To achieve this, you need to let go of the conservative tendencies most people unconsciously adopt when they become successful.

In my case, I keep tackling extreme sports like downhill mountain biking, motorcycle racing and car racing. These pale in comparison to the terror I felt earlier in life when I conquered public speaking and cold calling, but they are fortifying nonetheless.

Tackling your fears forces you into a vulnerable state. You're temporarily weak. Talentless. You're a novice again, learning from masters.

You will remember what it is to be mediocre, and how to scramble your way to excellence.

When you emerge victorious from a vulnerable state, it changes your psyche.

You're stronger. More resilient. You've fed your soul. This is how new heights of confidence are created.

Simple Summary

Keep challenging yourself to stay humble and hungry.

~~~~~~~~~~~~ *STORY* ~~~~~~~~~~~~

My grandmother Betty Howatt started university at the age of 81.

A bright, hardworking and engaging woman who was constantly learning, she and my grandfather were life-long entrepreneurs who owned a number of businesses across Canada.

What stands out to me most when I think back on my grandparents is how they were always up to something new; always tackling some new venture or challenge.

So I wasn't entirely surprised to hear that my grand-mother – who was forced to quit school in grade 11 – was pursuing higher education in her twilight years.

She told my mom that she intended to study religion, and its impact on society throughout history. She had a mind for deep topics. My mom described her as a 'real reader', the kind of woman who consumed serious books for leisure.

Betty died at 84, only three years after she started university. I guess you could say it was her last, great challenge.

When I need a push, a bit of inspiration, I think of my mother who told me – not once but 1,000 times – to 'just go for it'. (Guess I know where she got that from!) And then I visualize my grandmother who let nothing stop her: not the challenges of business, and certainly not her age.

To me, she is a shining example of pushing your limits, and living life fully.

~~~~~~~~~~~~~~~~~~~~~~~~~~~~~~~~~~~~~

Four Steps to Mastery

1. Know what worked in the past

Everyone has a history of pushing personal limits. These are the moments in life when you thought, "I may fail miserably at this, but dammit, I'm trying it anyway." Or when you had to struggle to get good at something new because you were in way over your head.

Make a list of the challenging times in your life when you pushed yourself hard, stood on new ground, and became more confident. How did you grow from each situation?

CHALLENGE	HOW YOU GREW
1.	
2.	
3.	
4.	
5.	

2. Create a Stretch List

Often people want to stretch themselves, but without a clear plan it doesn't happen. So make a plan.

Write a Stretch List, and include all the things you'd like to do to grow as a person.

This is kind of like a bucket list, but with a more directed intention. It doesn't have to include dramatic things like raising millions of dollars for charity, or summiting Everest – although it might.

Maybe your list includes mastering action photography, learning the guitar or becoming a certified SCUBA instructor. Maybe you want to meditate in silence for 10 days, or learn Spanish. Could be that you want to overcome your fear of snakes (did that!), or to speak in front of 100 people.

The specifics are up to you, but you need to select things that truly stretch you. Each one needs to make you uncomfortable.

Include things you would love to do simply for the exhilaration of it—and the fears you would love to conquer.

Action

Fill out the first column on your Stretch List.

STRETCH LIST

I'D LIKE TO...	LOCAL GUIDE
1.	
2.	
3.	
4.	
5.	
6.	
7.	
8.	
9.	
10.	

3. Find local guides

Learning has two currencies: time and money. You could invest thousands of hours to become proficient in a new area—reading books, watching YouTube videos, and learning through trial and error. This is a valid and rewarding way to learn for some people.

Because your life is already so busy, it may help to leverage the mighty dollar, and hire experts to help you tackle your Stretch List. Kind of like local guides, these experts already know the terrain, and can speed up your learning process.

So consider finding a photography teacher, taking a meditation class or signing up for private Spanish lessons. For me, local guides are always the way to go when I want to learn new things for work or life. My son and I recently joined a go-karting team for this reason. We get expert driving instructions and tech support for our go-karts. And believe me, it's a good thing we did. There is much more to karting than meets the eye. I now understand why it's the starting point for so many Formula 1 drivers. Anyway, I find experts make it easier for me to broach new areas. I'm less intimidated, and that means I try new things far more easily.

This is another great reason to hire a coach for business and life matters. Depending on the challenge you tackle, a coach may be a great guide.

Action
Fill out the 'Local Guide' column on your Stretch List to indicate where you would like a guide.

4. Just take a step forward. It's never too late to start

Like jumping into a cold lake or making a phone call you dread, waiting doesn't do you any good. You need to just do it, and you can be pretty much guaranteed you'll be glad you did.

Even if it isn't your nature to try new things, stretching yourself is a habit that can be learned. People that know me as an adult raise an eyebrow when I tell them I was a painfully shy, hesitant child. But it's true. I didn't arrive on this Earth the adventurer I am today. I have my mother to thank for the transformation.

She often saw a look of tentativeness (or outright terror) in my eye about doing things other kids were seemingly overjoyed to do. Each time, she would gently coax me into action by saying these words: "Just go for it."

Those simple words taught me to push through my fears. They helped me brave social situations, try a variety of sports, and generally understand that people are capable of far more than we think.

When my maternal grandmother went back to university at the age of 81 to follow a passion for religious studies, I learned another lesson. Age doesn't matter.

You can make bold, personal leaps at any age, and be a better person for it. Too many people hit middle age, and settle into a singular way of being. Radical new endeavours might be contemplated, but never pursued. _In the end, you will regret living this way_. So don't. Somewhere inside you there is a voice saying, "Just go for it." Listen.

Action

Which item on your stretch list calls out most for you to just go for it?

_____

You Need to Work on This if...

1. In the past six months, you haven't once thought, 'How the heck am I going to make it out of _this_ alive?!'
2. In the past 12 months, you haven't tried something new, and been a spectacular failure.

3. If a challenge makes you squeamish, you're likely to back down.
4. You haven't recently felt like the least competent person in a group.
5. There is something you would love to try if only someone could teach you.

Gut Check
How good are you at regularly stretching your personal limits? On a scale of 0 (low) to 10 (high): _____

17

Plan, Plan and Plan Again

"Everyone has a plan 'till they get
punched in the mouth."
MIKE TYSON, Prize Fighter

Planning and re-planning are two of leadership's most fundamental and underutilized skills.

Everyone from Steven Covey and Oprah Winfrey, to your own mother, will tell you if you don't know where you're going you're never going to get there.

Time is finite. You need to know exactly where to invest your hours and energy to get the results you actually want. You need to know which opportunities to focus on now, and what to let go or mark for the future.

Without a plan, it's far too easy to get distracted and focus on too many things at once, spreading your efforts thin and achieving fewer goals.

My approach to planning is distinct. I believe you need to have a single-page Master Plan for your entire reality – including work, self and life.

Long-winded plans are tucked into drawers and forgotten. Plans that include only your business goals and have nothing to do with self or life get you exactly what you would expect...a solid business and a haphazard, lacklustre life.

A simple, all-encompassing work-self-life Master Plan synchronizes all aspects of your reality, to make sure you reach for a bigger vision...*an amazing business or career <u>and</u> an amazing life.*

Key Point
Have a simple, all-encompassing one-page Master Plan for work, self and life.

Like all great plans, your master plan must start with a long-range view – your ultimate, big picture vision. Then, you can map out appropriate mid-range and near-term goals that lead to that vision.

Now, new information and ideas will come your way. Life will occasionally sock your plan in the gut. Because of these realities, *quarterly re-planning is absolutely crucial.*

Every quarter, take stock of new information, learning and ideas. Set next quarter's goals from a present-time perspective. This is your chance to course-correct. It's your chance to be strategic. And it's your chance to bring your long-term vision into the context of your everyday life.

Three Steps to Mastery

1. Commit to annual planning

For your annual planning, use the *My Master Plan*[*] worksheet to:

1. Review and reflect on your work, self and life results from the previous year.

2. Set long-range big picture goals for work, self and life based on your ultimate vision of an amazing life.

3. Set mid-range objectives for work, self and life that lead directly to your long-term vision.

4. Set annual goals for the coming year for work, self and life that lead directly to your mid-range goals.

5. Plan your focus for the quarter:

   a. Do the Oxygen Self-Assessment, which can be found at: *lawrenceandco.com/books*. Pick one of the 17 habits to hone and practice in the coming quarter.

   b. Pick your number one project for each quarter of the upcoming year. Why only one? The more things you commit to each quarter, the less likely you are to succeed at any of them.

6. Every year, repeat this process. Forever more.

---

[*] *You will find the Master Plan and Quarterly Reset worksheets on the pages that follow. Digital versions are available at lawrenceandco.com.*

ANNUAL REVIEW

HOW DID THE YEAR GO?

YOUR WORK Career, money, and investments	YOUR SELF Being happy, strong, and healthy	YOUR LIFE Friends, family, and community
Your biggest wins or achievements of the year?		
Your biggest challenges, frustrations or disappointments?		
The biggest lessons from your mistakes?		
PASSION RATIO: How did you invest your energy this year?		
___%	___%	___%
What would have been ideal for you to be your best?		
___%	___%	___%
If you could do the year over again, what would you do differently?		

MY MASTER PLAN

THE THINGS THAT MATTER MOST

	GUIDING VALUES	**SWEET SPOT** To Spend 90% of Your Time In	**WON'T DO OR TOLERATE**

	YOUR WORK Career, money, and investments	**YOUR SELF** Being happy, strong, and healthy	**YOUR LIFE** Friends, family, and community
The Ultimate in Your Lifetime			
To Achieve			
To Enjoy or Experience			
To Be Remembered For			
Twice As Good In 3 Years			
Passion Ratio	___%	___%	___%
#1 Objective			
#2			
Achieve This Year			
Passion Ratio	___%	___%	___%
#1 Goal			
#2			

QUARTER PLAN

PLAN FOR QUARTER ____ OF ____

	YOUR WORK Career, money, and investments	**YOUR SELF** Being happy, strong, and healthy	**YOUR LIFE** Friends, family, and community
Passion Ratio	____%	____%	____%
#1 Project			
Other projects?			
#2			
#3			
Toads #1			
#2			
Habit To Start*			
Stop			
Actions to take this week?			

* Choose 1 of the 17 habits from this book.

3. Re-plan quarterly

Use the *Quarterly Reset* worksheet toward the end of each quarter to:

1. Review and reflect on your work, self and life results from the previous quarter.

2. Plan your focus for the coming quarter.
   a. Do the Oxygen Self-Assessment. Here's that address again: *lawrenceandco.com/books*. Pick one of the 17 habits to hone and practice in the coming quarter. You might work on the same one a few quarters in a row until you see the progress you want.
   b. Decide your #1 Project for the quarter based on the newest and best insight you currently have about what will help you achieve your annual goals for work, self and life.

3. Repeat the process

Re-plan every quarter for three quarters, until it is time for annual planning again.

QUARTERLY RESET

REVIEW OF QUARTER ___ OF ___

YOUR WORK Career, money, and investments	YOUR SELF Being happy, strong, and healthy	YOUR LIFE Friends, family, and community
Biggest achievements?		
Biggest challenges or disappointments?		
PASSION RATIO: How much energy did you invest this quarter?		
___%	___%	___%
What would have been ideal for you to be your best?		
___%	___%	___%
What do you need to Start or Stop doing to be on track with your Annual Goals?		

QUARTER PLAN

PLAN FOR QUARTER ____ OF ____

	YOUR WORK Career, money, and investments	**YOUR SELF** Being happy, strong, and healthy	**YOUR LIFE** Friends, family, and community
Passion Ratio	____%	____%	____%
#1 Project			
Other projects?			
#2			
#3			
Toads #1			
#2			
Habit To Start*			
Stop			
Actions to take this week?			

* Choose 1 of the 17 habits from this book.

Simple Summary

Your achievements will be greater and you will enjoy life more if you make proper planning and re-planning an annual and quarterly discipline.

You Need to Work on This if...

1. You create elaborate, long-winded plans that you infrequently reference.
2. You aren't consistently achieving the goals you envision.
3. You get side-tracked by sudden inspirations and rogue projects that take you away from your true priorities.
4. You consistently overachieve in one area of your life (probably work) and feel you are sacrificing too much in other areas.

Gut Check

How disciplined are you about planning and re-planning?
On a scale of 0 (low) to 10 (high): _____

Parting Words

Standing still kills great leaders.

You can't be the same person you were six months ago, and deal with the challenges your business presents today. You need to be a new person, evolving all the time, continually stepping forward to meet your new reality.

In this way, high-growth leadership is like walking up the down escalator. If you don't take the next step, you slide backward. Staying in the same place isn't an option. You can only move ahead or regress.

The intensity of this commitment isn't for everyone, but when it's for you, you know it.

This book is written specifically to guide you on this journey, with the aim that you keep coming back to it over the years, to continue to strengthen yourself and to build the habits required to be a masterful leader.

I would love to hear the stories of your leadership journey. I invite you to send anecdotes, suggestions, techniques and tools that work for you.

I will end this book with the very same quote I began, with the genuine wish that you live your version of an amazing life:

"Life should not be a journey to the grave with the intention of arriving safely in a pretty and well preserved body, but rather to skid in broadside in a cloud of smoke, thoroughly used up, totally worn out, and loudly proclaiming, "Wow! What a Ride!"

HUNTER S. THOMPSON

Additional Resources
from Coach Kevin

Visit *lawrenceandco.com/books* where you will find tools, insights, videos and other resources related to this book including:
- The Your Oxygen Mask First Toolkit
- The Oxygen Self-Assessment

Be sure to check back regularly—I'll frequently add more resources.

Coach Kevin's Top Book Recommendations

1. *Art of War*, Sun Tzu
2. *Built to Last*, Jim Collins & Jerry I. Porras
3. *Blue Ocean Strategy*, Kim/Mauborgne
4. *Clarity: Clear Mind, Better Performance, Bigger Results*, Jamie Smart
5. *Confessions of the Pricing Man*, Hermann Simon
6. *Crucial Conversations*, Patterson/Grenny/McMillan/Swiztler
7. *Daily Rituals: How Artists Work*, Mason Currey
8. *Death By Meeting*, Patrick M. Lencioni
9. *Deep Work*, Cal Newport
10. *Execution*, Ram Charan
11. *Getting More*, Stuart Diamond
12. *Good to Great*, Jim Collins
13. *Great by Choice*, Jim Collins
14. *Great Game of Business*, Jack Stack
15. *Hide a Dagger Behind a Smile*, Kaihan Krippendorf

16. *High Output Management*, Andrew S. Grove

17. *How the Mighty Fall*, Jim Collins

18. *How To Win Friends & Influence People*, Dale Carnegie

19. *Influence*, Robert Cialdini

20. *Islands of Profit in a Sea of Red Ink*, Jonathan L.S. Byrnes

21. *Meetings Suck*, Cameron Herald

22. *Multipliers*, Liz Wiseman & Greg Mckeown

23. *Now! Discover Your Strengths*, Marcus Buckingham

24. *Radical Candor*, Kim Scott

25. *Rookie Smarts*, Liz Wiseman

26. *Scaling Up*, Verne Harnish

27. *Scrum*, Jeff Sutherland/JJ Sutherland

28. *Start with Why*, Simon Sinek

29. *Team of Teams*, McChrystal/Collins

30. *The 5 Dysfunctions of a Team*, Patrick M. Lencioni

31. *The 7 Hidden Reasons Employees Leave*, Leigh Branham

32. *The Five Temptations of a CEO*, Patrick M. Lencioni

33. *The Lean Start Up*, Eric Ries

34. *The One Minute Manager*, Kenneth Blanchard & Spencer Johnson

35. *The Only Way to Win*, Jim Loehr

36. *The OZ Principle*, Roger Connors

37. *The Power of Habit*, Charles Duhigg

38. *The Ultimate Question 2.0*, Fred Reichheld

39. *Think and Grow Rich*, Napoleon Hill

40. *Topgrading 3rd Edition*, Bradford D. Smart or WHO, Geoff Smart

41. *Tribal Leadership*, Logan/King

42. *Turn the Ship Around*, David Marquet

About Coach Kevin

CEOs typically place their first call to Coach Kevin with a crisis to solve. They stay because of his business acumen and no-holds-barred, tell-it-like-it-is style.

Kevin's career spans 20 years and four continents. He's worked with hundreds of CEOs and executives, helping them to break through business challenges, grow their companies and find personal success along the way.

These experiences inspired Kevin's book, Your Oxygen Mask First, in which he reveals the 17 habits every leader must know to transcend the perils of success, and achieve even more.

Kevin is a Coach Emeritus with Gazelles—a rare distinction. He is a key contributor to Scaling Up (Mastering the Rockefeller Habits 2.0).

Based in Vancouver, Canada, Kevin can often be found tearing up the racetrack, or adventuring in the outdoors with his wife Angela, son Brayden and daughter Ashley.

About Lawrence & Co.

We don't do best practices. And we are not for the faint of heart.

We offer real, unvarnished insight and tools based on 20 years of actual business experience, working with some of the world's most successful high-growth companies.

We cut through fear, time-wasting and abstract theories to get our clients to sound strategies, strong balance sheets and optimal profitability.

We believe in ease and simplicity, because complexity is over-rated and inefficient.

If you want a phenomenal business and an amazing life, get in touch.

Lawrenceandco.com